The Poetry Review

The Poetry Society, 22 Betterton Street, London WC2H 9BX

The Poetry Review

The Poetry Society, 22 Betterton Street, London WC2H 9BX
Tel: +44 (0)20 7420 9883 • Fax: +44 (0)20 7240 4818
Email: poetryreview@poetrysociety.org.uk
www.poetrysociety.org.uk

Editor: Maurice Riordan
Production: Michael Sims

ISBN: 978-1-900771-82-5 ISSN: 0032 2156
Cover illustration Shout / Dutch Uncle

. . .

SUBMISSIONS

For details of our submission guidelines, please visit the *The Poetry Review* section of www.poetrysociety.org.uk

ADVERTISING

To advertise, visit poetrysociety.org.uk or contact Robyn Donaldson on +44 (0)20 7420 9886, email: marketing@poetrysociety.org.uk

BOOKSHOP DISTRIBUTION

Central Books, 99 Wallis Road, London E9 5LN, UK. Tel: 0845 458 9925 or visit www.centralbooks.com

PBS EXCLUSIVE BOOK SUPPLY SERVICE

Readers of *The Poetry Review* can receive many of the books featured in the magazine post-free by mail order from the Poetry Book Society. To order, tel: +44 (0)20 7831 7468, Mon-Fri, quoting *The Poetry Review*.

SUBSCRIPTIONS & SALES

UK individuals: £34 / Europe: £44
Rest of the World: £49
(all overseas delivery is by airmail)
Single issue: £8.95 plus postage.
Order from www.poetryreview.org.uk or contact Paul McGrane on +44 (0)20 7420 9881.
Pay by cheque (sterling and US dollar cheques only), credit card or Direct Debit.

The Poetry Review is also available on audio CD.

The Poetry Review is the magazine of the Poetry Society and was first published in 1912. A subscription to *The Poetry Review* is included as part of membership of the Poetry Society. It is also available from leading bookshops. Views expressed in *The Poetry Review* are not necessarily those of the Poetry Society; those of individual contributors are not necessarily those of the Editor.

Charity Commission No. 303334

Supported using public funding by
ARTS COUNCIL ENGLAND

CONTENTS

Poems

Prose

Poems

Poems inspired by Germany Divided

The Geoffrey Dearmer Prize 2013

Reviews

Prose

EDITORIAL

*T*ee-hee, Carol Ann Duffy was quoted as saying when she walked off with the Forward Prize for *Mean Time* in 1993. It was the age of innocence. The 'Forwards' were on their second lap and it was the inaugural year of the T.S. Eliot Prize. These awards came with promotional savvy and glamorous presentation ceremonies, supplanting such discreet honours as the Alice Hunt Bartlett Prize and the John Llewellyn Rhys Prize – both now defunct. Never mind the razzmatazz or that the poets were put on beauty parade, this culture of prizegiving seemed a good way of supporting impecunious writers.

A couple of decades on, the prizes are looking rather tarnished. In Joey Connolly's measured appraisal for this issue, it appears they are held in low regard within the profession, with doubts about the efficacy and even fairness of the selection process. The time has come maybe to polish up their reputation.

We owe literary prizes to the Greeks. The annual Dionsyia held in Athens lasted for five days and were colourful quasi-religious events. They were closer in spirit to the Festival de Granada – reported on in this issue – than to Hay-on-Wye. Bulls were slaughtered, *phalloi* carried in procession, libations poured. The victor was crowned with ivy, which was sacred to Dionysus and chewed as an entheogen. The festival was devoted mainly to tragedy. Aeschylus, Sophocles and Euripides each triumphed on several occasions.

In classical Greece to be a winner, whether in the theatre or the stadium, was to achieve apotheosis, to partake, if only briefly, of divinity. You see it in the Charioteer of Delphi, the posture restrained but the mouth slightly agape, the gaze ecstatic: "this one came to me in a vision, this young Hermes", as Cavafy's "sculptor" might have said.

Our modern prizes are rooted in the profane ground of sponsorship and publicity. And they have proved an effective advertisement for poetry. Witness the two-thousand-plus audiences for the Eliot readings at the Royal Festival Hall every January. The competitions themselves, however, need to be run on principles of good practice, with clear rules concerning declarations of interest, and transparency about the process. It's not right to ask people to make career-changing judgements without proper guidance. And how to pick the judges – for integrity or for celebrity? Those Athenian arbiters sitting in the front row preferring the Sophocles to the Euripides were chosen by lot. Now there's a thought.

The danger with poetry prizes, however admirable, is that they create a poor measure of success. One need only scan old lists of awards – even indeed of Nobel laureates – to see how the enthusiasms of the *zeitgeist* may wane in a generation. But poems that last have the capacity to be refreshed with each reader. They thrive in the hours of solitude and surrender, in those encounters when the "house was quiet and the world was calm".

Such victories keep the tradition of poetry alive and require a mysterious blend of vision and craft. If you have the chance to step around that famed Charioteer at Delphi, you see the sculptor's most subtle achievement was in shaping the feet: imperfectly symmetrical, the muscles strained, almost tangibly active, balanced, and bearing the figure's weight.

Maurice Riordan

PHILIP GROSS

The Players

Somewhere in a square in the old world, by the Hotel Princip,
    by the Palace of Justice, somewhere in a park
        of clean gravel and poodle-cut trees

beside cobblestones seamed with tramlines, somewhere near
    a kiosk café whose waiter, in stubble and butcher-
        striped apron will fail to appear,

sometimes for days, at three wrought iron tables, bearing
    coffees concentrated to a fierce point, a black
        hole – one sip will suck you in,

turned to sparkling stone... Somewhere like this they sit, two
    old men, each one older than the other.
        Bending forward, they sit at a pace

from which the three-lane traffic is a shimmery smear,
    a mirage, oil on water, and the pieces
        themselves seem a fidget,

a jitter of cause and effect which leaves no choice but,
    now and then, to lift a hand... a moment's
        late appraisal, as the world

turns one more orbit. One
                moves. Looks up. The other
    nods. I've seen them at the black and white
        marble table with the raised squares

in the Garden for the Blind, a table like a plinth
    on which they are building ice sculptures
        of certain uncertainties, and

it is beautiful, very, they might say. If ever they spoke.
    (Kibbitzers do the chatter for them.) They
        live, if indeed they do,

in twenty worlds at once, all intercutting: *if, and if*
    not, then, and if then, not... Every
        thirty years or so, a bang:

slammed door or backfire of exhaust, and now and then
    a handgun. All the combinations shatter
        into flight, up

over rooftops, dewlapped gables, weather vanes
    to reform, circle, circle, homing
        on wherever we may be.

Ways to Play

Simultaneously. Blindfold. As an exhibition.
Lightning. Quick death. In bed, by candlelight,

with you, naked. In the original Persian.
For hours, for weeks, on a mind-blanking cruise.

In a tent, in the rain, in the mud. In a cream-
coloured caravan, with kids, in desperation.

On a red and white plastic travel set, tiny,
queasy, in the back seat of the car. To please

mum and dad, though not equally. Not –
that would be unlikely – to impress the girls.

Online, against names who might be any
body, age or sex. Against a deep machine.

For a place in the ratings. Face to face
with yourself, and solo, with the board

against a mirror. With human-sized pieces
played by loudhailer from a first-floor balcony.

To absent yourself from bruising playground games.
In a trench, in a foxhole, on the night before.

In reverse, to lose, where losing's winning.
With grave diplomacy, in place of war.

To take on an aura, like a psychiatrist's
accent. Or a Viennese beard. Because sense might be made

within sixty-four squares. Professionally.
With ruthless insouciance. Yes, to win, or to win

a reprieve. Because what smarter way is there
to lose? For escape. For the side. For your soul.

On Poetic Form: A Short Essay

The form stands in the corner of the room
like a man made of glass. All he can be
is how the light bends through him; he's the way
reflections and refractions play, the zero sum
of its deflections and distractions. *Come
on in*, I say, as if there was a he
to speak to, or an I to speak, or words to say
or any other place to come in from

except time. How many rooms have held, might hold
him, he them – had their décor rearranged
in his impartial gaze? He makes me feel old
and young (not in a good way) and yet... *Chance
it*, he says, silently, and everything is changed.
He never moves, and yet we start to dance.

SUSAN UTTING

The Journal
after Song Dong

The first week was in ink,
broad-nibbed black, each day
a slope to the right, the thin
and thick of copperplate.

The second week was fog
and muffle, a slowing down
of daily round, a 4B graphite
exercise in evening.

Week three was smudgy,
began with charcoal across
sugar paper, then washed
its hands of dark for good.

Week four was scratched
with a pin on wood, each letter
purpled-in with laundry marker,
each day a table-top tattoo.

Then I took up my brush,
dipped and wrote with water
on to stone: letters rippled,
grew to words, to stories.

Years now, stone has held
what I have written, has worn
itself away with listening – water
whispers for me, stone never tells.

EDWARD BARKER

Drop

To think that young mind, unrecognisably mine,
carried the frescoes of Knossos inside it.
And Zyklon B. One to the other. Palaces and ovens.

All while the sea rolled its pinpricks of light
again and again like a gambler throwing it all
regardless. Then with the flood tide

came thorn-hairs, half-jobs, years on barbs,
on barbs., the fugue of distillery chimneys,
gangways rotting and falling away in the hands,

and longing all the while for the unobtainable,
its slow calcifications, the body feeling its way
towards love and unlove,

up to the rank smell of the returning shore
as it works over seaweed and jellyfish domes
in this last pewter light. Above, below,

and all around is the well.
No drop ever echoes. The absence of sound
is like waking out of being awake.

SARAH HOWE

Sirens

pickerel, n.1 – *A young pike; Several smaller kinds of N. American pike.*
pickerel, n.2 – *A small wading bird,* esp. *the dunlin,* Calidris alpina.

I see it clearly, as though I'd known it myself,
      the *quick look* of Jane in the poem by Roethke –
that delicate elegy, for a student of his thrown
      from a horse. My favourite line was always *her*
sidelong pickerel smile. It flashes across her face
      and my mind's current, that smile, as bright and fast
and shy as the silvery juvenile fish – glimpsed,
      it vanishes, quick into murk and swaying weeds –
a kink of green and bubbles all that's left behind.

I was sure of this – the dead girl's vividness –
      her smile unseated, as by a stumbling stride –
till one rainy early-evening, I met an old friend
      for a drink across the road from Magdalene.
We passed under The Pickerel's painted sign,
      its coiled fish tilting: *oldest pub in Cambridge.*
Our chat fell to Roethke, his pickerel smile, and
      I had one of those blurrings – glitch, then focus –
like at a put-off optician's trip, when you realise

how long you've been seeing things wrongly.
      I'd never noticed: in every stanza after the first,
Jane is a bird: wren or sparrow, *skittery pigeon.*
      The wrong kind of pickerel! In my head, her
smile abruptly evolved: now the stretched beak
      of a wading bird – a stint or purre – swung
into profile. I newly saw the diffident stilts
      of the girl, her casting head, her gangly almost
grace, puttering away across a burnished mirror

of estuary mud. In Homer, the Sirens are winged
      creatures: the Muses clipped them for their failure.
But by Renaissance, their feathers have switched
      for a mermaid's scaly tail. In the emblem by Alciato
(printed Lyon, 1550) the woodcut pictures a pair
      of chicken-footed maids, promising mantric truths
to a Ulysses slack at his mast. But the *subscriptio*
      (author and draughtsman didn't confer) denounces
women, *contra naturam*, plied with the hindparts

of fish: *for lust brings with it many monsters.*
      Or take how Horace begins the *Ars Poetica*,
ticking off poets and painters who dare too much:
      their special licence to mate savage with tame or
snakes with birds can only create such horrors,
      he says, as a lovely woman's body that winds up
in a black and horrible fish. What breed of poem
      is this? I was never clear if he's complaining
here of too much imagination, or not enough...

The girl in the poem, or rather her smile – swimming
      through my mind's eye's flummery like a game
of perspectives, a corrugated picture: fish one way
      fowl the other. Transmuting from winged nymph
to siren, and back again. Could it be that Roethke
      meant the word's strange doubleness? *Neither father
nor lover.* A tutor watches a girl click-to the door
      of his study with reverent care, one winter evening –
and understands Horace on reining in fantasy.

Stray Dogs

Thou art a beaten dog beneath the hail
    – *Pound*, Canto LXXXI

To think again of Pound, bared to the sky at Pisa.
The traitor's cage they built for him specially. 6 x 6 ft
of airstrip mesh & dust. Wire diamonds running
even underfoot. Day 25, the DTC doctors transfer him
to a medical tent (*A swollen magpie in the fitful sun*)
fearing the first signs of a breakdown. Three weeks i'
this here sun goan change a man, thinks Mr Edwards
(he with the face *of the Baluba mask*) as he flips over
a packing crate, hang reg'lations, to fashion the traitor
a writing table. Squat at his crate-cum-desk, Pound
spreads flat the worn-out covers of his dog-eared
Confucius: he'd slipped it in his slacks' side pocket
that day at the house, a rifle butt pounding the door.
As he flicks through the *Analects*, his hand starts to
tremble. He pushes it hard into his temple. Takes up
the donated pencil stub: *Pull down thy vanity.* Near
illegible. Scrawling on squares of shiny latrine roll
now lodged in a library's vaults. Later he gets hold
of a G.I. pad, ruled lines turned ninety-degrees
like bars. No longer blithely ranting on Rothschilds
as in his radio days (*Whether they are born Jews
or have taken to Jewry*). Circe's sty. Glorious cant.
Our captive flutters again to the much-thumbed page
where, having lost his disciples at the city's east gate,
Kung takes with equanimity the stranger's slur:
"Look at this man here, he has a face like a lost dog!"
"Yes," smiles Kung Fu-tzu, "yes, that's quite correct."

Banderole

diminutive of Fr. *bannière*
used in war of a lance's
streaming flag; in art,
the resourceful painter's
only means to make
mute canvas speak –
whereby a tawny scroll's
unfurling coil will stretch
self-involutedly away from
a boot-faced shepherd's
startled lips exhaling
their small consternation
at deity – a breath that lifts
beribboned & scripted
in the age's neat blackletter
to signify the silent noise
– a Latinity beyond
his own lacked letters –
of the frozen man's half-joy
half-penance – its skyward
path a virgin's curl
or trumpeting pennant –
up, and further up, into
how a Northern painter saw
the scumbled heavens
one midwinter

ALAN GILLIS

The Scattering

Gone through the half-hearted window
that gives like a watery eye
onto the East, the blushlight of dawn
on scuzzed rooftops, scrolled hills;

gone over open-mouthed duck ponds,
decked lawns, a populace dreaming
of ordinary sex; gone with limitless texts
through the gridded air's dataflow,

the wheesht of elm leaves in the air,
fingers rustling a blue polyester blouse;
gone with lost souls, their children
photostreams in the cloud,

indebted and encased in metal
and the motion of their cars past yellow
fields, roundabouts, the dead everywhere;
gone into the excitation of particles

and elements in contact with other
elements and particles, like peedie
heads in a primary school playground
rushing away from fathers, mothers:

as I turn away, face the room I'm in,
half of me is already out the window
to chase and meet the scattering day
heading West, as if to say, well, hello.

River Mouth

If some regions of the brain are foreign
to others, as they say, this might explain
why my moods swing like hips in a hula dance:
now grumped, now chipper, now the essence
of cement, now a gushed river flow.
A woodland river. Green, brown and yellow
limn its banks: sprunt pines and bending sycamores,
song thrushes. It rushes for the shore
the way that urge surged through me, out of my mouth
in sounds not half my own, when I burst forth
into song this morning in the kitchen.
There was no reason to sing. No one to listen.
Happiness comes on like a once-loved song
on the radio – played over in the mind once it's gone.
Useless to follow. It doesn't end, doesn't start:
a river that twists and turns into the unsatnaved heart
of the woods which shift in their shade perpetually,
sunlight pooling in the heads of the trees,
while a congregation of sound fills the air,
pulls the ear. Useless to ponder where
that happiness went to, where it had been:
I can't even catch the dark-yellow-light-brown-flecked green
while I follow the many-voiced river through downs
and drumlins, rail stations towards the border of town,
past warehouses, vast retail lots, car-stained
miles of suburban families detained
in dream homes. To apprehend such density
of life would be to hold fresh to memory
each page of each book on a full forty-foot shelf.
The mind can't keep up with itself
and I get lost in town – masonry changed by whims
of weather, helter-skelter buildings on thin

streets huddled together: granite and whinstone,
polished ashlar, red sandstone, blonde and brown stone,
many-sized windows numerous as rain-
drops in the air: each an eye cast on this drained
world; each an eye giving onto an inner
realm I peer into, staring at the décor
of strange rooms, going "ooohh", "yuk", or "hmm?",
catching a glimpse of a grey cluttered room:
a woman at a desk, rubbing her aching neck,
her tired eyes, turning away from her book,
laptop, stacked plates and cups, scribbled words,
turning away from this tasked world towards
an inner realm – her thoughts quicksilver shoals
in motion through a green water-blue soul –
her eye a twilight moon over this wood's
gushing river I follow under the mood
swings of sycamores, fearful of the pines,
wondering where on earth does the time
go while the weather turns and cold winds
ruffle the witch-hazel, rustle the whin,
wilting sweet gum. Smokebush withers.
Woodland thins. Crows caw and circle
the blush sky, mild above autumn's
mown fields, borderlands, foreign regions
where the river, many rivers, empty
into a dark sea, the mind of nobody
where whatever it was that was borne in song
floats and dims on the brim of meaning.

MICHAEL LASKEY

Weighing the Present

I didn't believe it for a minute
but turning the corner at the lights
saw him waiting on the opposite pavement
outside A1 Discounts to cross.

Though I didn't believe it for a moment
I knew it was him by the set
of his shoulders and head, that physique
and the all but forgotten lift

of my heart at the sight of him.
For an instant he was alive
or I had died, though I knew
neither could be true and pressed on

to the post office past my friend
with the present that needed weighing,
more or less knowing nothing
was impossible, even heaven.

Together

Even when I rub her back
in bed sometimes, when my hand
curves over a shoulder blade
or the tips of my fingers affirm
her warm breathing skin and follow
the course of her vertebrae down
the long valley of her spine;
even then, so close to her all
but inaudible sigh of wellbeing,
I miss her, I grieve for her, ache
for the small of her back I'm actually
making much of, stroking – better
pull yourself together, mgl.

JOHN F. DEANE

Ark of the Covenant

Already another year
is touching on high tide; winds
have been raising waves across the swollen meadow;

clouds grey and white and grey again
bunch up, like summer crowds on the slow road
home from the shore. Love made covenant with me

these decades back, days on the riverbank
when trout responded to stick, twine and pin,
with woodbine fragrant after rain; I ran then, laughing,

from the scuttling forays of the white
farmyard geese. These later times I might expect
a flood of huge proportions, to purge us of the wars we wage

on the good earth, who have grown smart
with chemicals and missiles, though we hold to prayer
that love's unaltering generosity might keep us safe: as Noah

and the remnants of all flesh
stood out one dawn on washed ground, smelled
the fragrance of woodbine after rain, and saw love

light up again
in all her promise
the dreary undersides of the clouds.

The Ruined Meadow

Something of the reassurance of the seasons in it,
a tractor
out in the meadow, mowing; evening, high-sky blue,

and then the tractor going on through darkness,
headlights
sending fence-post shadows through the window;

they moved across the kitchen wall,
unholy shapes
shivering in a timeless silence. By morning

bales of light-green grass littered the shorn field.
Pigeon on the chimney-pot
hoo hwhoo hooed his love-call of sustained distress

echoing where the smooth presenter of this day's deadly news
spoke his own hoo hwhoos
into electric air. Syria, he said, the children… and stuttered

into silence. And then – billions of years in its fostering,
perched now
on the sheep-wire fence – there he was, robin, *spideog,*

with that engaging look-you-in-the-eye cockrobin-ness,
small chubby masterpiece,
created out of air and the plucky verve of spirit, plaything

of a fierce universe, reassurance, too,
in that sharp eye,
taking ownership of the mist, feasting in the tractor ruts.

CARRIE ETTER

Song a Year After My Mother's Death

I allowed a small song
to nestle between my breasts.
It was furtive, a ground squirrel
occasionally checking the wind.

I thought it could not grow
on wine and despair. It didn't.
On the one sunny day in a rainy month,
it basked.

It took on colour: peacock blue
shimmering like sunlit sea. I feared
it would strut. I watched
it fly forth

afraid of no one, no one
but me.

Overheard in Chicago

"I'm not narcissistic. I'm not bipolar."
I have a sister who's both, but have
Four siblings and you can have expectations

Of illegitimacy, jealousy and one changing friend.
Rain and snow precipitate self-loathing,
A kind of self-love, perhaps. I'm not bipolar.

I have four sisters: Fate, Hope,
Death and Pandora. You can imagine
My expectations, illegitimate as I am.

Just drive two hours south to find
The lot, well settled in the Town of Normal.
Let's not talk about the weather.

SIMON ARMITAGE

Kitchen Window

You wanted more view, more day. So out
came the heavy sashes and bevelled frames,
the dulled, soft-focus cataracts of old glass,
the counterweights – dumbbells of crude iron
hanging on frayed ropes – all thrown in the skip.

Wrapped in a canvas sheet the brand new pane
rode on the side-rack of the joiner's van.
Undressed and carried, the cloudscape tilted
in its mirror and the planet swayed, though
set in place it seemed a solid nothingness –
a panel of air or frozen light
that magnified its own transparency.

Simian, almost, in nature and name,
I could swing up onto the outside ledge
and hunch in the angle of wall and lintel,
my ankle hooking a plastic bucket –
a lukewarm broth of bloated sponges and cloths,
and a slimy liver of chamois leather
for swabbing the glaze.

                From inside the house
the hummingbird of your hand and finger
pointed or tapped at streaks and smears, or your face
came close to the brink to mouth instructions
then fell away behind a net curtain.
Then fell away further, sinking to deeper
darker reaches, and would not surface.

Camera Obscura

Eight-year-old sitting in Bramhall's field,
shoes scuffed from kicking a stone,
too young for a key but old enough now
to walk the short mile back from school.

You've spied your mother down in the village
crossing the street, purse in her fist.
In her other hand her shopping bag nurses
four ugly potatoes caked in mud,

a boiling of peas, rags of meat or a tail of fish
in greaseproof paper, the price totted up
in pencilled columns of shillings and pence.
How warm must she be in that winter coat?

On Old Mount Road the nearer she gets
the smaller she shrinks, until you reach out
to carry her home on the flat of your hand
or your fingertip, and she doesn't exist.

OMPHALOS

*I would begin with the Greek word, omphalos, meaning the navel, and
hence the stone that marked the centre of the world, and repeat it, omphalos,
omphalos, omphalos, until its blunt and falling music becomes the music
of someone pumping water at the pump outside our back door.*
                                         – Seamus Heaney, 'Mossbawn'

> *As part of an occasional series, we ask poets to write about their
> omphalos, a place central to their imaginative world.*

· · ·

Simon Armitage

I came into contact with poetry at school, when I was fifteen or sixteen,
but began thinking in poetic terms several years before then as a result
of a domestic reshuffle in our house. I grew up in a two-up, two-down
end-terrace, and there came a time when my older sister needed our
shared bedroom for herself. So a small corner of my parents' room was
annexed off with sheets of chipboard, and I packed my things and made
the one way journey across the landing. The room was L-shaped because
it had to accommodate the bulk-head over the stairs, and ridiculously
small; with a wardrobe and bed inside there wasn't even enough room to
fully open the door. But it gave me my own space, my own daydreams,
and the chance of keeping my own hours. More importantly it gave me a
window, and one that looked out over the village. From now on I had a view.

Travelling west into the Pennines from Huddersfield, Marsden is the last village in Yorkshire. And Wood Top felt like the last house, perched on a steep single-track road that carried on into the moors and the sky. My new window looked down into the bowl of the village, into its workings and clockwork operations. At one stage I kept a log book, recording the colour and make of vehicles as they circulated the system, and the comings and goings of local characters passing between houses, shops and pubs. The fact that Marsden is ringed on three sides by moors, quarries and hills only increased the sense of theatre, the feeling of enclosure and enactment, of the village as a crucible or one of those snow-globes where events took place in miniature yet were magnified under the lens of curiosity and observation. That window, I believe, became the template for all my future poetry, an almost literal frame which mimicked the shape of the page and provided an ongoing creative perspective. Marsden became my Llareggub, my sweet Auburn, even my Greenwich Village when I tried out New York School poetics against the terraces and mill walls, and listened to the warped linguistic echo that bounced back. Tens of dozens of my poems look out through that window, from the very first, 'Snow Joke', to the last poem I published, 'Emergency', about the defunct fire station and the demolished petrol garage. More recently, to write two poems about my mother – one from the high field behind the house and one looking into the kitchen at street level – I made the epic journey around the gable-end from the front of the house to the back, an expedition of about twenty-five feet.

. . .

Gwyneth Lewis

My *omphalos* is all radius and no centre. It covers over seventy per cent of the globe. Mostly it's a no-man's land, though ribbons of it are claimed by nations. For all that it's a friend, it will kill you as soon as look at you. The ocean takes us away from 'here' but leads us right back, having circumnavigated, to ourselves. Some physicists say that the universe has exactly the same geometry. Sometimes I get so tired that all I can bear is the sound of waves breaking, saying nothing. A repeated sigh. A body nearby.

I've stood on the physical *omphalos* of the Holy Roman Empire in Hagia

Sophia, Istanbul, and tried out the thought, "I'm the king of the castle". I wasn't. Being translingual, I've lost all belief in the monolithic. I thought I spoke one language, but it turned out to be at least two. My Welsh-language primary shared a playground with an English-language school. Children are tribal and there were scraps.

My father rode his bike to work for the Public Health Department in Cardiff docks. I'd wait for him at the top of the hill, so that he'd put me on the crossbar for the long coast down to our Wimpy house in Heol Gabriel. Later, when he had a car, he'd take me on calls – to an abattoir or a warehouse. In the port, I recall horrific black grease coating rails, cranes like giant toys and, in the distance, however gloomy the day, a silver glitter, the glint of an eye.

Coming from a port city, you can't but know that language is a mode of transport and not a destination. In the Trinity, between the father and the son are the wings of the holy ghost, like a stretching and contracting body of water. My favourite Welsh hymn, written by Gwilym Hiraethog (William the Longing), tells us: "Here's a love as large as oceans / Mercies tender as the sea." The sea's a place that connects others. It's the landscape which makes me understand the basics of metaphor. As in the Greek meaning of the word – to transport – each metaphor carries meaning like cargo between places. I can't separate the sea from that field which changes space and time. It's the nowhere that gets us all to somewhere.

Every poet's sea has a different character. Here's Seferis in his 1946 journal:

> The unexplained magic of the sea. How quickly it changes me; this is my amazement, deep amazement, in my very bones. I can't understand. I must go nearer, cross this line of separation into another world.

Even as he dreams of his lost friend, Arthur Hallam, Tennyson's poetry voyage combines music and danger:

> And while the wind began to sweep
> > A music out of sheet and shroud,
> > > We steer'd her toward a crimson cloud
> > That landlike slept along the deep.
> > > > > > (*In Memoriam*, CII)

Only in a poem can you safely steer towards the facsimile of land without risking shipwreck. We carry the sea in our bodies. Aimé Césaire's ocean is a dangerous intimate:

> *Le sang du monde une lèvre salée*
> *vertement à mon oreille aiguë*
> *sanglote*
> *gréée de foudres*
> *ses fenaisons marines*

> The blood of the world a salty lip
> rigged with lightning
> sobs sharply
> its marine haymakings
> into my keen ear

(trans. Clayton Eshleman and Annette Smith)

It was inevitable that I should learn to sail and, at some point, run away to sea. Seamanship's an art of balancing forces: wind against tide, the angle of a sail against the keel. For, as a German captain reminded me once, "Always you are sailing over graves." It's easy to become spooked at sea because you're never the boss. One night, before we went on our longest voyage – as far as North Africa – my husband and I moored our boat to the Milford Haven tugs' buoy at the entrance of the harbour. I woke up in the middle of the night and went on deck. The waters were at rest but uncanny, teeming with light, even the land was flowing. Anything could have happened. And then it did.

Essay

AT THE CHOSEN EXTREME
Conor O'Callaghan

T he last work of the Reverend, Learned and Holy Mr Richard Baxter, puritan theologian of Kidderminster of the late seventeenth century, is his *Dying Thoughts*. An abridged version, running to about two hundred pages, remains widely available. Heaven alone knows how long the full-length edition of *Dying Thoughts* was. But one can reasonably deduce that the Reverend was not quite so close to death as he had initially supposed.

Geoffrey Hill has, you could say, made dying his life's work. From the very outset, his every phrase and line has seemed squeezed from extremis, the limits of speech, the brink of extinction. He has been doing it for sixty years now. *Broken Hierarchies*, collecting all of Hill's work from the earliest composed poems of his first collection, *For the Unfallen*, to his most recent 'daybook' dating from 2012, has the air of prolonged deathbed musings. Even his most celebrated lyric, 'September Song', famously deviates from meditation on the death in Terezín of a near contemporary into parenthetic self-requiem:

> (I have made
> an elegy for myself it
> is true)

It is hardly necessary, of course, to quote these lines. Everybody knows and quotes them. But they remain deliciously indicative of all the young Hill was and did: the ornate artifice of the address; the air of the confessional's whisper which the brackets lend; the deliberately stilted enjambment, enhanced by the phantom comma between the last two words of the second line, which seems to mimic a dying exhalation; the whiff of gallows humour implicit in the very fact of punctuating a Holocaust poem with such an apologetic navel-gazing aside. It is all Hill can do, you feel, to suppress a smile before permitting the horror to resume. 'Funeral Music', the sequence of blank bloody sonnets on the Battle of Towton, is ultimately "Dragged half-unnerved out of this worldly place, / Crying to the end 'I have not finished'."

Both of those passages are culled from poems in arguably Hill's finest individual collection of small lyrics, *King Log*. The book dates from 1968. What an old soul he must have seemed: publishing soliloquies and fantasias and baroque meditations on England's religious wars and history's "speechless dead", while the Beatles were releasing *The White Album* and the students rioted in Paris. Already, you suspect, an unflattering caricature was forming of him as tortured, cloistered prig ignoring the realities of his immediate political moment.

"Exquisite, immaculate music." The description belongs to Michael Longley. He was right. Before anything else, Hill was and remains the son of a Bromsgrove police constable; the grammar school offspring of "obstinate, outclassed forefathers", one who would never forget the value of education, the power of knowledge, the measure and weight of every chosen word. His visual and ethical imaginations were formed by the wartime landscape, and his attention has always been tuned to the deeper historical undercurrent as opposed to any surface noise. In *Mercian Hymns*, arguably his masterpiece, the solitary boy-poet gets conflated with a Dark Age king. Contemporary references are precious few; its contemporaneity is established, rather, by the formal movement of gorgeous modernist prose stanzas. Here and elsewhere, the work is informed by rather than merely about; the phrase-making is saturated in those nuances which words tend to appropriate with time. The opening stanza of one of a staggered sequence from the 1990s, for example, goes:

Aspiring Grantham
rises above itself.

Tall churches wade the fen
on their stilts of glass.

('Dark-Land')

This is about Margaret Thatcher, isn't it? She was, after all, Grantham's most celebrated daughter, the age's great evangelist of social betterment and upward mobility. One can only savour that "spire" at the core of "aspiring": how the word establishes immediately the modest scape of a market town glimpsed remotely across flat fields, and how the more obvious pun of the second line serves to augment that conceit. There is even a crash audible in the shimmers recasting as "stilts of glass".

By *Tenebrae*, his last substantial collection before a twenty-year period of something approximating silence by contemporary standards, the output had grown thin in terms of basic volume. Revisiting those early books, the scarcity starts to look like fasting in the face of language's guilty excesses. There is a natural overlap between the theme of English sovereignty and Hill's spare religious rhetoric. What gets less frequently noticed, it seems to me, is the overlap between his poetry's religious dimension and its command of the erotic: its play of soul and body, the aching tension between penitential hunger and carnal satiety. When all of these elements coalesce, it results in a hard-won simplicity as surprising as it is visionary:

Goldfinch and hawk
and the grey aspen tree
I have run to the river
mother call me home

the leaves glint in the wind
turning their quiet song
the wings flash and are still
I sleep in the shade

when I cried out you
made no reply
tonight I shall pass by
without a sound

('The Pentecost Castle')

Beyond that, it seems pointless to paraphrase great work from what is now another age. Those who know it know its worth. They will, like me, bemoan the excision in this new volume of those marvelously tortured notes which accompanied original publications; the more cramped typography, most grievously with a three-sections-per-page bludgeoning of 'The Pentecost Castle'; the inclusion of eighteen new 'Hymns to Our Lady of Chartes' not half as swoon-inducing as the original three; the proliferation of new epigraphs tagged unnecessarily onto old poems. And those latecomers for whom Hill remains "an alien landscape"? Read those titles named above, plus the spoof-translated laments of 'The Songbook of Sebastian Arrurruz' and 'The Turtle Dove'. They represent, to this day, the best of Hill and should be counted among the imperishable glories of twentieth-century poetry. If their beauty does not speak to you, then he is not for you. Plain and simple.

Thereafter the floodgates open and the waters muddy. What to make of Hill's second coming? The most obvious thing is its sheer volume: the 1985 Penguin *Collected* represents 160 of the 940 pages of the present volume, or, putting it another way, he has published almost five times more in the past thirty years than he did in his first thirty years. The figures themselves are meaningless, but they do suggest a dramatic shift of approach if not of broad thematic concerns. Where the early work is distinguished by its clenched, melancholic perfectionism, those recent volumes seem wilfully more carefree and, at times, careless. In a disarming interview with the *Paris Review*, Hill has openly credited his recent prolificacy to America and "happy pills", to what section LIX of *The Triumph of Love* calls "the taking up of serotonin". It has to be recalled that this return happened not only after a decade's silence, but also at a time when he was *persona non grata* within British poetry. In those high years of New Gen leftist vernacular pentameter, the Hill mode could not have been more out of favour. The bitterness of that period becomes, at times, too pronounced, not least in the petty cracks about "Swedish millionaires" (Heaney? Walcott?).

The figure of Eugenio Montale is crucial. *Without Title* is dedicated *in omaggio* to his Genoese forefather. Elsewhere, there are six competing versions of 'Il gallo cedrone' ('The Capercaillie') and a vignette of Montale post-war in Ely cathedral "visiting England in the off-season... a depressed man's orison". Most memorably, there is a beautiful translation of 'La bufera' which underlines, via the consonantal re-enactment of nature's "harsh buskings, bashing of castanets / and tambourines around the spoiler's ditch", the audible impression that Montale's fragmented cadence has made in Hill's.

But it is not simply the echo within particular lines of a certain '*decenza*'. Montale also, clearly, provides a model for the trajectory of Hill's more recent publishing. After three sporadic collections which secured his centrality to twentieth-century Italian poetry, Montale's second incarnation came in the 1960s and 70s with a series of poetic diaries and one notebook ('*quaderno*') which lack, arguably, the finish and rich visual dimension of the great early work. His poetry became more frequent, querulous and throwaway. Ditto Hill, who has used Montale's example to recast himself as garrulous waspish joker, a purveyor of 'daybooks'. Hill seems to admire, indeed to find kinship in, Montale's aloof refusal of fashions or orthodoxies, be they right or left, Communist or Catholic, and the solitary remove held in both writing and life. He openly admits as much in a passage which provides the plainest statement-of-intent that Hill has ever made, and a key (or 'code') to his recent output:

> It surprises me not at all that your
> private, marginal, uncommitted writing
> – this is to be in code – came at the end
> to the forum of world acclaim
>
> [...]
>
>   [Internal
> evidence identifies the late
> Eugenio Montale as the undoubted
> subject of this address.]
>
> [...]
>
> I admire you and have trained my ear
> to your muted discords.

A se stesso... Literally, 'to himself'. The phrase, which comes down to us primarily via Leopardi, occurs many times as a refrain in the second half of *Broken Hierarchies*. As with Montale and Eliot (to whom Hill is equally indebted), there is a 'you' permanently hovering in the wings, an elusive interlocutor who could be an other or simply one of the author's many selves. The net effect is a series of book-length sequences which, cumulatively, sound like an old man alone in a room depopulated but for literary shades, throwing voices, whooping and clapping and chuckling at his own allusive barbs.

More than anything, Hill seems to rejoice in his status as outcast, as "shameless old man" railing against the crasser aspects of our age: the internet, political doublespeak and even heavy metal for heaven's sake. Five books, from *The Triumph of Love* to *Without Title*, are a veritable torrential tempest of italicised quotes, Hopkinsian stress-marks, locked-cap 'headlines', spoof editorial interventions in square brackets and rhetorical questions. Long-haired, Lear-like, at once consumed by rage and delighting in folly, Hill leaves it all out on the heath of his own isolation.

At times, the fury feels both justified and compelling. The clownish note results in lots of authentic belly-laughs: "Sir, your 'Arts / Life' column claims that Gracie / Fields sang in Dunkirk. Is this / a misprint? For sang read sank?" At other times, it gets too like being in the company of some learnèd geezer who insists on reading aloud from the newspaper solecisms that exemplify the decline of our moral fibre. Oy vey... Just when one – the otherwise sympathetic reader – feels compelled to chuck said doorstopper against the nearest stone wall, something resembling the old sorcery flickers on the horizon, a clarity so intensely moving as to be worth the bilge-wading: a certain English landscape, say, or the erotic glimpsed again from decrepitude, or that age-old refrain regarding the hopelessness of simple utterance:

> Wintry swamp-thickets, brush-heaps of burnt light.
> The sky cast-iron, livid with unshed snow.
> I cannot say what it is that best
> survives these desolations. Something does [...]
> (The Orchards of Syon, XXVIII)

And there are still four hundred pages to go: the half-rhyming quatrains of *Expostulations on the Volcano* and *Al Tempo De' Tremuoti*, the sapphics of *Odi Barbare*? Take your pick... Alongside Montale and Milton and Bonhoeffer, Hill adds to his private hall of fame such improbable exemplars as Hart Crane and Jimi Hendrix. In another interview, he has even acknowledged the influence of Ken Dodd. Shape-throwing fancy though that sounds, there is an undoubted hint of music hall in much of the humour: the puns grow ever more clunky, in a manner that can only be intentional; section 48 of *Ludo* concludes: "I / say / I say I say "; and the accumulative self-conscious verbosity is reminiscent of The Chairman in the BBC's 1970s variety show *The Good Old Days*, pausing between each polysyllabic gobstopper to allow the stalls to cheer or barrack:

Posthumous retroactive vocations
Contriving bric-á-brac and *scarabrie* [...]
`   (*Expostulations on the Volcano*, 14)

Smudge-typed Admirality communiqué
Pronouncing valediction: in dense skeins
        Of frozen spray
Corvettes raw-reeving through Icelandic day.
                          (*Clavics*, 26)

Gwalia hostage to insatiable
    Swoln rhododendrons.

Goldengrove notebooks ripped for late bequeathing;
Dyscrasy Publike its own gifts to plunder [...]
                          (*Odi Barbare*, XL)

Etcetera. Dashed allusive stuff, all told. Which segues neatly into the 'difficulty' issue. This is the routine criticism of Hill's work: it is not accessible. The man himself will argue, and has done so eloquently many times, that this is not a credible aesthetic yardstick. And in this regard he is surely correct. We judge municipal buildings by their accessibility, not poems. But the issue of difficulty gets too tritely centred around literal comprehension. Do you understand what it means? If not, it is difficult. What if you do understand its meaning? The educated reader of the present journal, for example, is likely to 'get' swathes of this. Does getting enough of the myriad cross-references, however, make the work any less difficult? There are surely ways for poems to be difficult other than basic sense, be they tonal or rhythmic.

For my part, I find much of Hill's version of bricolage, his flarf-before-the-fact density of allusion, makes for dispiriting and frequently tedious reading, whether I understand it or not. Hill has always been a bookish poet. But in the very best of his work, those many influences form only part of a greater historical inheritance, remain merely ways of mediating a world that is still being seen and felt. Now, there appears to be almost no world other than others' words. Perhaps inevitably, for a man in his ninth decade, he has receded into memory's echo chamber. His ear, to be frank, has largely gone. I can only repeat something the youngish Larkin, reviewing *Homage to Clio*, complained of the aging Auden: "He has become a reader rather than a writer", with "literature... replacing experience as material for his verse".

Once, in an essay on Hopkins, Hill upbraided the diction of something Donald Davie wrote for being "richly allusive rather than 'pure'." It always struck me as a curious distinction, as if allusion/purity were natural antonyms. In the intervening decades, Hill has come around to absolute impurity, and clearly has no further ambitions for "exquisite immaculate music". At some point our favourite poets stop being the poets with whom we fell in love, and we have to forgive them for that. We have to be grateful that he is still among us, still doing it, and trust that the spate of interest in his newer work will lead fresh readers back to *King Log*, *Mercian Hymns* and *Tenebrae*. Titled, fêted, scarcely a week goes by without some journo declaring Oxford's current Professor of Poetry as "the greatest living English poet". Is he? There are younger English poets producing better poems than Hill is currently writing, sure. But none out there has written anything that could hold a candle to his best. Like Montale, he too has "come at the end / to the forum of world acclaim", and no living poet deserves that more than Geoffrey Hill.

Geoffrey Hill, Broken Hierarchies: Poems 1952-2012, *OUP, 2013, £35*
ISBN 9780199605897.

Essay

THE SCANDAL OF DYLAN THOMAS

Gwyneth Lewis

D ylan Thomas is most identifiably Welsh in his evocation of the twenty-four strict metres of medieval Welsh *cynghanedd*, or harmony. This form of poetic display makes alliterative Anglo-Saxon versification look like *vers libre*. With its tradition of extreme word-play, using a combination of one or two pauses in the line, combined with accentual, consonantal and rhyme patterns, it insists on word music as an abstract as well as concrete art. Here's a line-by-line analysis of a Dafydd ap Gwilym poem from the fourteenth century:

> Dewin fy nhŷ // a'i dawnha,
> D   n   n ´//   d   n ´
> Dwylo Mai // a'i hadeila,
> D ´ l˘(m) ´ //   d ´ l˘
> A'i linyn yw'r gog // lonydd
>   l´n˘n   (r g g)// l´n ˘
> A'i ysgwîr // yw eos gwŷdd,
>   sg   //   s g

This is poetry as fractals before they came to light, as well as being a theory of the word as central to the whole of creation.

In order to write in *cynghanedd*, you have to attune your ear to the skeleton of words – that is, the consonants – and arrange them in corresponding pairs. Then you also need to delight in vowels, the flesh around the bones of words, so that you may rhyme them internally and at the ends of lines. You also need to have a feel for where accents fall, in order to rhyme stressed with unstressed syllables. All these effects can be found in Thomas's work, in lines like "knocked in the flesh that decked the vine", "Hang a ram rose over the rags" and, most famously, "Though I sang in my chains like the sea."

Such intricate patterns require some homework. Here's a notebook entry, an index of words related by sound:

> *Flick, fillip, flip, fleck, flake.*
> *Flick* means to touch or strike lightly as with the end of a whip, a finger etc. The *fleck* is the next tone above *flick*, still meaning to touch or strike lightly (and leave a mark of the touch or stroke)... Key to meaning of *flick*, *fleck* and *flake* is that of striking or cutting off the surface of a thing; in *flick* (as in to flick off a fly) something little or light from the surface, while *flake* is a thin scale of surface.[1]

The list-maker isn't Thomas, as you'd expect, but one of his poetic fathers, Gerard Manley Hopkins. When Hopkins was a Jesuit novice at St Beuno's College in North Wales, he studied Welsh *cynghanedd* with a local woman. Thomas's parents spoke Welsh but he didn't. However, through his West Walian relatives, he would have been aware of the sound of Welsh and the melody of Welsh prosody. However, I think that Thomas learned his *cynghanedd* not from his family but from Hopkins.

Thomas's relish for complex form is a characteristically Welsh taste. Like his contemporary, Euros Bowen, he practised a form of *cynghanedd* liberated by a modernist sensibility, giving us a new, exciting sound:

> After the funeral, mule praises, brays,
> Windshake of sailshaped ears, muffle-toed tap

---

1. The Journals and Papers of Gerard Manley Hopkins, *ed. Humphry House, completed Graham Storey (OUP, 1966), p.11.*

Tap happily of one peg in the thick
Grave's foot, blinds down the lids, the teeth in black,
The spittled eyes, the salt ponds in the sleeves,
Morning smack of the spade that wakes up sleep,
Shakes a desolate boy [...]

(*CP*, p. 73)

It has been fashionable to dismiss Thomas's music as a result of his inebriation on language. Not only is this stereotypical thinking, it's plain wrong. It denies his ferocious intelligence. In a letter to Richard Church, he insisted: "every line *is* meant to be understood; the reader *is* meant to understand every poem by thinking and feeling about it, not by sucking it in through his pores, or whatever he is meant to do with surrealist writing" (*CP*, pp. 211-12). 'I, in my intricate image', as Vernon Watkins points out, has seventy-two variations on the sound of "i" in line endings, twenty-four in each part. This is the height of Thomas's clotted style – metrical difficulty as obsession. Even here, he wasn't privileging sound over sense but using words in an abstract way, seeing them both as words and things at the same time. This is one of the reasons his work gives such physical pleasure in the mouth. In later poems, influenced by his broadcasting, he began to speak more directly to his audience.

The Welsh tradition offered him both stimulating and less helpful models. Because his parents chose to call him Dylan Marlais Thomas, it could be said that the poet was born into Welsh mythology. In the medieval tales of the *Mabinogion*, Dylan Eildon (Dylan of the Second Wave) is a strange lost boy who, as soon as he was born from his unmaternal mother, headed for the sea – which is a vivid presence in Thomas's work. He was, I believe, at the end of his life going to use the early Welsh poet Taliesin as the model for his projected sequence, 'In Country Heaven'. The sixth-century Taliesin is the original shape-shifter in the Welsh tradition. Here's Taliesin, in Rowan Williams's translation, saying how he's moved through creation in numberless shapes:

Before my release:
A slim sword, enchanted...
A drop in the air,
The sparkling of stars,
A word inscribed,
A book in priest's hands.

Thomas wrote that he planned to write a long poem in the character of

> The godhead, the author, the milky-way farmer, the first cause,
> architect, lamplighter, quintessence, the beginning Word, the
> anthropomorphic bawler-out and blackballer, the stuff of all men,
> scapegoat, martyr, woe-bearer – He, on top of a hill in Heaven.[2]

Thomas-as-Taliesin is more than a shape-shifter, he's God himself: a
dangerous persona for a mortal to adopt. This is especially true if, as
Thomas was, you're both an atheist and a Puritan.

He displays a religious reverence for language:

> such sand-storms and ice-blasts of words, such slashing of humbug,
> and humbug too, such staggering peace, such enormous laughter,
> such and so many blinding bright lights breaking across the just
> awaking wits and plashing all over the pages in a million bits and
> pieces all of which were words, words, words, and each of which
> was alive forever in its own delight and glory and oddity and light.[3]

This belief in the immortality of language contrasts with his early, simple
relationship with words:

> Once it was the colour of saying
> Soaked my table the uglier side of a hill
> With a capsized field where a school sat still
> And a black and white patch of girls grew playing [...]
> (CP, p. 74)

Elsewhere, words are scarecrows – not the goal of a search, but merely
symbols to distract scavengers from the real goal of the poet, the crop
around the figure. 'Once it was the colour of saying' continues that, having
grown up, the poet's work is to dismantle that vision of language as
innocent:

---

2. *John Goodby,* The Poetry of Dylan Thomas: Under the Spelling Wall *(Liverpool:
Liverpool University Press, 2013), p. 400.*

3. *Ed. Walford Davies, Dylan Thomas,* Early Prose Writings *(London: Dent, 1971), p. 156.*

> The gentle sealides of saying I must undo
> That all the charmingly drowned arise to cockcrow and kill.

He's suggesting that the poet can raise the dead. The end of the poem has no illusion about the cost of this project:

> Now my saying shall be my undoing.

This is the moment where we see Thomas box himself into the contradiction that led to his later troubles. As with all writers, his life followed his writing, not the other way around.

More than any other writer, Thomas's career and reputation illuminate the falsity of the dichotomy posited by W.B. Yeats between a poet's life and his or her art. Take this story about Thomas, which I found in a curious book called *The Miracle Stone of Wales* by Marguerite Caradoc Evans (under the name of Oliver Sandys). Her husband, Caradoc Evans, a satiric prose writer, was one of Thomas's heroes. The seventeen-year-old poet went on a pilgrimage to visit him. The book tells the story of a stone, which, according to the dust jacket, was given to "the authoress... by an old Welsh shepherd, who wished only that as many people as possible might benefit from its healing rays." On a visit to the Evanses, Caradoc sent the young Thomas up to wish on the stone:

> "Wishes?" Caradoc took him up quickly.
> "I had three wishes."
> "Asking too much."
> "They are all joined together, three in one, like the Trinity."[4]

The couple met Thomas years later when "he had coarsened and his features were thickening already". Caradoc asked the poet if his wishes had come true:

> Dylan removed clinging tobacco flakes from the moist loose lips between which a cigarette had been dangling.
> "Not likely. I asked for fame, success, money."[5]

4. *Oliver Sandys,* The Miracle Stone of Wales, *(London: Rider & Co, 1957), p. 53.*
5. *ibid, pp. 53-4.*

Thomas was a scandal in the religious sense of the word. The concept comes from the Latin *scandalum*, "a cause of offence or stumbling", and the Greek "a trap or snare for an enemy, cause of moral stumbling" (*OED*). As Andrew Davies's bio-drama *A Poet in New York*, depicting events before Thomas's death, showed recently, the spectacle of a poet behaving like a madman has lost none of its popular appeal. The story's a scandal in that it has both settled into an orthodoxy about the romantic figure of the poet but has hindered reception of his work. The discredit Thomas brings on his vocation can hardly be described as his fault but gossip is a more attractive endeavour than getting to grips with Thomas's brand of modernism.

In November 1953, Elizabeth Bishop wrote with distress about having lunch with Thomas and Joe Frank, the biographer of Dostoevsky: "I said to Joe later something trite about 'Why he'll kill himself if he goes on like this,' and Joe said promptly, 'Don't be silly. Can't you see a man like that doesn't *want* to live?'... But his poetry has that desperate win-or-lose-all quality, of course – and... eliminates everything from life except something almost beyond human supportability after a while."[6]

In his great thundering poems, 'And death shall have no dominion' and 'Do not go gentle into that good night', he denies the reality of death with hammer blows of will and rhythm. Such a position, though, gives the poet nowhere to go except into his or her own poetic abilities. I've recently had the experience of watching my own father die, while I was reading Thomas's poems closely. I've come to the conclusion that no child would wish a parent not to go gently into death. 'Do not go gentle' is Thomas's elegy for himself.

Wales, with its traditional reverence toward the figure of the bard, encouraged Thomas to go further out on an artistic limb than was comfortable or safe:

> And from the first declension of the flesh
> I learnt man's tongue, to twist the shapes of thoughts
> Into the stony idiom of the brain,
> To shade and knit anew the patch of words
> Left by the dead who, in their moonless acre,
> Need no word's warmth.

6. Elizabeth Bishop, *One Art: Letters*, ed. Robert Giroux (London: Pimlico, 1994), p. 276.

The root of the tongue ends in a spentout cancer,
That but a name, where maggots have their X.
(*CP*, p. 22)

We admire those poets who have the courage to follow the language god to such lengths, even as we grieve their loss and, secretly, feel grateful that we can profit from Thomas's extraordinary journey, without having to undertake it ourselves.

At the end of his life, he was facing a crisis which all poets face, sooner or later. It's like being a golfer with an entirely natural stroke. You've been playing since you were a child without any coaching. However, what happens when the demands of the game at the highest level put pressure on an instinct that's served for so long? Baudelaire wrote about exactly this moment:

> I am sorry for poets who are guided by instinct alone; I consider them incomplete. In the spiritual life of great poets a crisis infallibly arises, in which they want to reason out their art, to discover the obscure laws by virtue of which they have produced, and to derive from such a scrutiny a set of precepts whose divine aim is infallibility in poetic production.

Unluckily for Thomas, this rite of passage coincided with a perfect storm of personal, health and financial problems. I have no doubt that, like a golfer whose game is demolished by a coach and then rebuilt on better principles, he would have managed the transition. Like all writers, he was constantly striving to write better than should, strictly speaking, be possible. Most poets, even those who survive to an old age, never manage to surpass themselves in the way Thomas had done, time and again, by the age of thirty-nine. Had he lived, the transition would have resulted in a fascinating addition to his body of work.

Based on talks for Poet in the City, 10 February, 2014, and for BBC Radio 3's The Essay, broadcast 7 May, 2014. Quotations of Thomas's poems are from Collected Poems, ed. Walford Davies and Ralph Maud (London: Dent, 1971).

The Dead Come Out in their Sunday Best by Sir Peter Blake © Peter Blake, 2014.

No Good Boyo by Sir Peter Blake © Peter Blake, 2014.

Rosie Probert by Sir Peter Blake © Peter Blake, 2014.

Dylan Thomas's centenary occurs this year. He was born on 27 October 1914 in Swansea, and died in New York thirty-nine years later on 9 November 1953. This year also marks the sixtieth anniversary of the BBC's production of Under Milk Wood. *Sir Peter Blake's illustrations of the play were first shown at the National Museum Cardiff and are now on display at Oriel y Parc in St Davids, Pembrokeshire, until 23 September 2014.*

JODIE HOLLANDER

Splitting and Fucking

1

My mother,
poor woman
somehow she was
always the victim
of splitting and fucking,
fucking and splitting.
For example
that last guy,
he was a split
personality.
He split all kinds
of things like
the front door,
Mother's flower
pots; once
he even split
her forehead open –
blood everywhere.
But mother said
he could fuck,
so she kept him around
until that time
he really fucked
up at the movies:
The Aviator
was playing that day,
something in that
must have set him
off, but who
knows with split

personalities.
Anyway,
He started kicking
her so hard,
Mother screamed –
It must have been
ear-splitting
because they stopped
the whole movie;
the police came
and took him away.
That's when my mother
finally split
up with that fucker.

2

After that
you would think
she'd had enough,
but then her body
fucked her over
big time –
mutant cells
splitting and fucking
all over
her insides.
Too late
for the doctors
to stop it –
stage four,
even chemo
was useless now.
Fucking cancer

taking my poor
Mother's life,
she was only
sixty-two
and already
had to pack
it all up.
But how would she
divide her things
amongst her children
and the neighbour,
and more importantly
who would get
the only thing
she ever loved
in this fucked-up world –
the dog?

FIONA MOORE

Numberless

Sometimes in one of those dreams
where everything is out of place
but only a little bit, only
a little surreal, the dreaming self
realises: oh, it was always
like that. The television did
always sit on the narrow work top,
bulging slightly. You always had
a green Paisley scarf that you'd knot
at your pyjama neck like someone
out of *Brideshead*. With a small
jolt of surprise and acceptance
last night I realised that a colleague
had waited forever down the road
in his car for me to direct him
through Greenwich, past the convent
skyscraper, 30s Chicago style,
purple granite, and say *mind the nun
and the other women*, one of whom
(his vestments covered with crosses)
was a priest and my dream-self
found it right to refer to him thus.
The colleague had always had
a snowstorm of stubble, which thickened
during the journey. It's as if
the dream is acknowledging
numberless permutations
of daily life, so our waking selves
don't need to, otherwise long ago
I'd have walked through the upstairs
bedroom window which leads,
by now, to many places.

City from a hill, through open windows

Listen to the silence
of eight million sleeping – curled, sprawled,
together or alone –
a counterpane of bodies, each
held in its own breath-filled cell. Not all
asleep. Each sleep
interlocks with the next: is this
what the dawn reveller shouts out against?

Our dreams are
London's underworld, our murmurs form
the backing for one wren
that crowns itself and the dawn with a song
repeated, repeated: echoed
distantly by another.

SEÁN HEWITT

I Sit and Eavesdrop the Trees

The woods are the organ
of the wind. The wind puts its hand

over the forest's mouth.
Trees struggle for breath, then faint.

It is a wood – it doesn't speak
except to itself. Its eyes are knots in bark

and it is April and it is moving.
I can hear the soft, transmuted

aches of growing and easing back
to form, the forest creaking awake

around me. Then nothing but mutterings,
the sun bending its neck to look through trees,

birds building houses from the open ribs
of bushes. My quick movements startle

the sleeping leaves. When I turn, things speak...
Now the wood swallows me into its heart,

pushing weather rings behind bark
in its old, megalith slowness. I hold still,

hearing nothing but the crackle
of my own ears opening.

It starts to rain. It rains. The still day
whispers with the feedback of dead leaves

like dust translating on the air's vinyl.
Hold your ear

to the ground: you can hear
the voices caught in the earth, chattering,

and the rain typing on puddles
and the wind wiping them clean.

Slitten Brook

The sleeping canal lies sleep-slow.
In the midnight hush, there is nothing
but the old tick of my bike-chain turning,

and a voice in Slitten Brook, its echo
opening through the trees, its spiral
reverberating and hollowing the wood.

At first it is wolfish, and I notice the moon
suspended over the houses, its one bright bulb
commanding the silence of the village.

But no, the voice calls in the wood, waking
the little secrets between the branches, twitching
the small eyes under the dry leaves.

A tawny owl has picked its way
through the taut arras of night and out
onto the black twigs high in the trees.

Its cry is aged and haunts the air it moves on.
Time is curled into the hollow note of its call.
I stop to listen. It's as though the owl's hoot

has tapped the tuning fork of my spine,
and I am back in the cold church of the wood,
picturing the appalled eyes, the ancient mask

hung up in the beeches whose leaves
flicker a light breeze. In its voice, I can feel
the knife-flint of the beak, the ungodly head twisting.

Woods in the Cold Light of Morning

A weird uncertainty of light, the sun's ghost
at the edge of the trees. Heaven-held
light. The branches are ladders from the night's
violet crypt. There is a silence held like a bell
in the eardrum as after the dreadful detonation.
Things crawl and drag themselves upwards
for the morning's nursing hand, the light,
out from under rotten arms of wood, from
rotten skins of lead. This morning, the sun
lifts and pries through the leaning spaces
of the trees, its light unpicking the lock
on the secrets of the wood. Everything holds still.
"Don't say anything," it whispers. "Don't speak."

HARRY CLIFTON

The gig with the golden microphone
Graham Bond 1937-1974

London, without you, is reinventing itself
Like a jazz musician. Another Spring
Atonal with birdnotes, and the promise of sex –
So Graham, wake from the dead and do your thing
On Hammond organ, alto sax,
And leave your linctus bottles on the shelf

Where they belong in the Age of Addictions.
This is posterity – to be clearheaded,
Orchestrating the music of chances
You blew in a lifetime. Send us your benediction,
Potbellied magus, fair game
For loansharks, dealers, wives on maintenance –
You went for a walk one day, and they found you dead.

It is a long time now since Nineteen Seventy Four.
Terrible how the world forgets, how the doors
Of the Brixton tube you flung yourself under
Open and close, and the ceaseless millions shuttle,
Dormant, mute, between brake and throttle.
Terrible the lost chord in the traffic thunder.

Blood was washed from the sleepers. Life went on –
Another age, another sound.
If you came back now, to hang around
Finsbury Park, all would be lights and clocks,
White magic, the Seven Sisters Road
Policed against streetwalkers, the mortar and bricks
Through which Johnny Rotten exploded.

If you came back now, it would not be too late
For Ladbroke Grove or Notting Hill Gate
To remember you. As for the rest,
All over London the players, the brilliant ghosts,
Have done themselves to death,
Demoralised... When it all comes together,

As one day it will do, Graham, show us a sign –
The stigmata of your healed veins
In the purifying waters of Shannon, or of Ganges,
Your victories on the astral plane
Against the musical warlocks with their black arts.
"There is no death, there are only changes"

You used to say, to whoever would pick up the tab.
Klooks Kleek, Flamingo, the old Marquee
Are gone forever. Climb in the cab
With your real instruments – soon it will be dawn
And the gig with the golden microphone
Waits for a New Age, in the druid hub
Of England, where your ashes have been sown.

MIKE BARLOW

I explain to my long-dead father how poetry is less authentic than dreaming

at which point he comes to a halt on our brisk
walk home through back streets, turns to me
and quotes, word perfect as if it were his own,
the elegy I'd struggled with for years.
Never a poetry man, he was more a reader
of maintenance manuals, so hearing my words
in his voice renders them methodical, didactic.
I stand there, dispossessed. He seems embarrassed
to have put me at a disadvantage and making
as if he's just remembered something, ducks
into a corner shop to emerge with a packet
of firelighters and an evening paper.
In the sort of silence only family can brew,
we proceed home, though in fact we're lost.

COLETTE BRYCE

Re-entering the Egg

Like some magnificent Swiss clock,
the house has been rebuilt
in the same position, in that Georgian street.
Tall and lean, it tilts towards us,
lists like a ship on rough seas
as it always did, only look (how clever!)
the front can be opened
with this small lever.

A tiny family fills the rooms.
In one, a wife is breathing fire,
genies whirling in the air.
In one, we hear the Strong Man's snores
rumbling under a mound of clothes
like a subterranean train.
In one, first floor, a spangled girl
enters in her diary: *I am headed for a fall.*
In one, girl-twins, conjoined
at the skull, freak themselves
to a pitch of shrieks, *A rat, I saw it! There!*
In one, a mermaid, washed up on the floor,
amber-lit in the notional glow
of a three-bar fire, strums a guitar,
hooks blonde hair behind one ear.
Like a baby bird re-entering the egg,
the smallest girl's soft breath
knits round her like a shell, like pearl,
where she's curled up sleeping
on the topmost bunk
of a creaking bed.

A television flickers blue
in another room
and a British voice reports the news
as smoke-rings loosen in the air, disperse,
and turfs collapse in the grate
beneath the glowing coal
in the ruptured chest
of the Sacred Heart.

Out of time, they go about their lives
unaware of our scrutiny.
Close it up. That's enough for now.

Positions Prior to the Arrival of the Military

Mother (out for the count) has been carried
from the ring. *Ding ding!* we have a victor,

Father, who has vanished in a puff of smoke
from his pipe, to return in the small hours.

Sister has stepped from her sleeping body
and floats about unnoticed amongst us,

a dream she will later recount,
while brother, who sleeps on the ceiling

lately, gazes down like a Sistine cherub
with a lute, a stain spreading on the sheet

where he used to sleep before
he was safe. The screen in the corner

has much to offer: heart-warming stories,
Little House on the Prairie.

Satellite beams are connecting all this
with New York, Bangkok, the Moon (in theory).

You're climbing the banisters, monkeying up
through the house without the aid of stairs –

a test, if passed successfully,
that will save the world from nuclear meltdown.

Rat-a-tat-tat at the door and the dog
is going berserk. All hesitate

Magic Eye

See him in the IRELAND baseball cap.
See her in a pair of too-large trainers
clowning down precipitous streets
to the special pub with the blacked-out panes
that no one else sets foot in, where only those
who have fallen through the cracks lie low.

They star in more scenes than you think,
take a look. Let your gaze relax
like Magic Eye, those pattern prints
where shapes might slowly surface. There
he lies: feel free to prod him with a toe,
put your mind at ease that, no,

he hasn't died. Inside his head
it is dark, a back road over the border
at night where a notional verge requires
great care and steps are perilous.
Their faces are breaking out of their faces,
livid red. When strangers clutch

her arm, concerned, or slap her cheek
and say her name, she sways to her feet
and stands before a hinterland
of rumour: kids in care, debts, abuse;
all of it called to explain why they kip
in boarded flats with rats or slumped

in a shop's entry, steaming where they lie.
They are up early, sit stunned
in a fizz of stars or flies and watch
the march of other lives to work,
managers raising shutters on the day,
bin men's sweep and clearance.

Their eyes, peeled in the morning sun,
though onion-raw, are looking in
towards some awful destination
to which each instinct is impelled
as needles drawn to north.
You blink, and find them gone.

Like you they lived their whole lives
in this town, their parts assured.
For that, perhaps, you should be glad
as you cross their path so hurriedly
in the shopping mall, and take your place
in line on the mirrored escalator, rising.

JACOB POLLEY

Nightlines

Jackself and Jeremy Wren are setting
nightlines in the kidney-coloured pool
all the streams of England run into
    Jackself's fretting
        all night they'll hang, their hooked lips
mouthing curses into the waterworks and bloodstreams
of all England
    all night, gaffed,
their bullion flexing
to no end but their own
which will be when Jeremy Wren
bashes them at dawn with his hardwood priest
    Wren, who says his granddad built the southern domes
Jesus needed to stable His beasts,
thinks Jackself's a soft-lad, a quick-
tear, a worry-wit,
and ties off another triple-barbed spinner
    Jackself rolls up his jeans,
takes one end of the nylon line, looped to a tent peg, and
wades into the chuckling shallows   slippery-stoned ice-cool
foot- and fish-path where no one has stood
for a thousand years   midstream
Jackself stamps
and all the perch and pike and trout,
the carp and stickleback, chub, roach, rudd and bream
are shivered out
of their lower heaven's muddy-minded dream,
knowing at once, as if all water's thought,
their own sweet metals' preciousness
and how to not get caught

Jack O'Lantern

the leaves are slimy yellow light
   the year's a sticky door
the wind bangs in the barest trees
   and shakes the apple core
       no   again   the leaves are slime
   the year a bloodshot eye
the trees the rooms of bedlamites
   with bars across the sky
the wind's inside the apple core
   the moon bangs like a drum
and   no   again   the sky's a door
   the year a slum
the wind a house of bedlamites
   with trees in every room
the leaves collapsed like junkie's veins
   and yellow light a broom
the moon's inside the   no   again
   the year breaks down the door
the leaves are shut inside the trees
   the trees in apple cores
the wind bangs in the barest rooms
   of bedlam   no   again
the leaves are rooms, the no   the moon's
   a   no   the year a vein
of narrow gold, the trees gold flakes
   the leaves gold leaves, the wind
a whiny   no   again   the rakes
   are brooms, the moon is skinned
and   no again   the bedlamites
   have wedged the no   again
the wind is bare and yellow lights

are banging on the brain
the year's wedged shut with apple cores
    the no a yellow stain
the slimy moon an open sore
    and every room the same

Swimmer

He swims through the dark
where there are no stars.

Whose dark has no stars?
The blind potato's
and the blinder stone's.

His breaststroke throws
up constellations of bones.

Poems inspired by Germany Divided: Baselitz & his generation at the British Museum, London, 2014

MICHAEL HOFMANN

Baselitz and his Generation
(for Hai-Dang Phan)

*"I have no doubt where they will go. They walk
the one life offered from the many chosen." – Robert Lowell*

*"They are all also, it should be remembered, West German artists, with
the partial exception of Penck, and are all male." – John-Paul Stonard*

He was born in the countryside / the provinces / the blameless sticks
     in (*false*) Waltersdorf (*recte*) Dresden
     in what is now Czechoslovakia / the Czech Republic (*laughs*) /
                    Czechia, if it ever catches on
     what's it to you.
Stripped of his East German citizenship, he fled
     on foot with a handful of pop music cassettes
     in a pantechnicon *mit Kind und Kegel*
     in pandemonium
     nach vorne
     cool as you like, in an S-Bahn from the Russian Sector, in the
                    clothes he stood up in.
Germany (thus Goethe's friend Mme de Staël) is the land of poets and
                    thinkers
     der Dichter und Denker
     or of judges and executioners
     der Richter und Henker
     or of Richter and Penck.
He drew innocent geometrical shapes
     boxed shirts / boxer shorts / boxy suits
     men without women
     hairy heroes of the Thirty Years' War / lansquenets / strangely
          fibrous figures a bit like those *New Yorker* caveman cartoons
     empty Renaissance helmets / mostly US fighter jets
     the suicides of Stammheim.

Adler (Eagle) 1981 by Georg Baselitz. Woodcut. From the portfolio *Erste Konzentration I*,
published by Sabine Knust, Maximilian Verlag, Munich, 1982. © Georg Baselitz 2014, courtesy of
the Trustees of the British Museum. Photo: Courtesy Archiv Georg Baselitz/S. Warmeser, Munich

He took the name of an American boxing promoter
    a German Ice Age geologist
    the village of his birth
    the one he was given.
His first work to really catch on / be banned / get him in trouble / cause
                                 widespread revulsion was *Onkel Rudi*
    Die grosse Nacht im Eimer
    Höhere Wesen befahlen: rechte obere Ecke schwarz malen! / *oyez, oyez,*
          oyez, Politburo decree: upper right hand corner in ebony!
    ohne Titel
    a mural in the cafeteria of the Hygiene Museum, since painted over.
He wound up in Düsseldorf
    Berlin, *doh!*
    la bella Italia
    tax-exempt Ireland of Böll- and Beuys-full memory, where the
                                     earth-apples bloom.
His paintings were fuzzy geometry
    like the country, ripped across the middle
    upside down (especially effective: the trees)
    shovelled out of the window
    later withdrawn.
His favoured technique involved stick figures
    Polke-dots
    out of focus *grisaille* photographs
    scribbling on his pictures
    woodcuts *a la* Dürer.
The numerals on his graphics represent a recent shopping bill
    an attempt to disconcert the onlooker / *Ostranenie*
    amortization
    barcode
    some other code
    Durchnummerierung.

He studied with Joseph Beuys
    the least doctrinaire painter he could find
    for the best part of ten years, in East and West, so that everything
                                        cancelled itself out
   what's it to you
   he didn't.

KATHRYN MARIS

The House with Only an Attic and a Basement

When two sane persons are together one expects that A will recognise B
to be more or less the person B takes himself to be, and vice versa.
> – R.D. Laing, The Divided Self

The woman in the attic did not have visitors.
The man in the basement gave parties that were popular.
The woman in the attic had mononucleosis.
The man in the basement had type 1 diabetes.
The woman in the attic listened to audiobooks which the man
    in the basement held in disdain.
The door to the attic swelled in some weathers; in order to shut,
    it had to be slammed.
"There is a way in which" was a way in which the man opened sentences,
    as in "There is a way in which to close a door so it doesn't slam."
The woman in the attic took cautious walks to build her strength.
The man in the basement pointedly said, "Some of us have ailments
    which are not manufactured."
The man in the basement wrote stories about heroin.
The woman in the attic read stories with heroines.
The woman in the attic noticed a bruise that ran from the top to the
    base of her thigh.
The bruise looked like Europe.
The man in the basement was in love with the sister of the secretive
    man who loved him more.
He whooped at the woman, "You killed your student?"
To himself he wept, "I killed my father."
The man in the basement, recently divorced, was left with literally two
    possessions.
The woman in the attic purchased books on psychopathology.
The man in the basement produced faecal matter
that blocked the pipes in both attic and basement.
The woman in the attic produced nothing at all.
The woman in the attic was a waste of space.

The man in the basement had sex almost daily.
The woman in the attic had panic attacks.
The man in the basement had only one rule:
the woman in the attic was banned from his bedroom.
But once she stole in and lay on his bed
in his absence (or perhaps he was absent because she was there).
The man in the basement moved to the West Coast;
the woman in the attic crossed the Atlantic,
whereas the house with the attic and basement saw states
of fumigation, exorcism, detoxification, and rehabitation.

Zwei Streifen (Two Stripes) 1966 by Georg Baselitz. Charcoal, watercolour & graphite on thin laid paper, Presented to the British Museum by Count Christian Duerckheim. Reproduced by permission of the artist. © Georg Baselitz, courtesy of the Trustees of the British Museum.

SAM RIVIERE

People say olives are best served on ice, but I like them room temperature, in brine, unless it's warm enough to eat outside. I begin in the top left corner and proceed from left to right, pretty much in the way you'd imagine. I prefer watercolours of sports cars to an oil painting of dead people hunting. I include two luminous figures and a huge, black, church-like interior. I support the early work that suppports an alternative reading. A figure of eight in the acres of parking. I'm not in favour of towns that bow down to their cemeteries. I sought my revenge in proxy realities. A nice panic attack in the midwinter market. My picture used to hang here, but I filled it in with block colour. This is the sixth reproduction. In practice it's costly, but it costs more than I spent. The moment I'm after is when one person in a crowd of thousands looks straight at the camera. Instead of a sentence you could just build a shelf. For the 40th time I died trying to break in to the collectors' convention. My city is custom, my language is custom, I built the maps from an ancient graveyard. I don't know my own number. I enjoy the music of ice cubes. When my prince came on a plane I heard his soft thunder. I searched for Los Angeles, and a few other places, but ended up here, in the one city they decided to raze. I relax by playing a stressful game. I want to see your side of the version. I praise the back of a painting. I see consciousness as a pond-shaped, deepening dip that I can feel myself occupy as I fall asleep. I had plans for words that never came to anything. I even had words for the storm's architecture. I copied your notes. They just use rain to erase the tall buildings. We're not so different, the system and me. With all the huge ads and bouts of consumption I felt like I was in Britain or something. The boys stand without moving in tiny white cubicles, still believing they're being considered. The youth all have that Aryan look. If the talk is too boring I like to imagine Levin's pioneering use of the acronym. When I'm cleaning a staircase I leave one step unswept, just to compare with. Everything I've ever loved fits in your silhouette. I get collector's envy. A glass breaks when I remember your name, but not because I remember your name. The shelves are all sanded, but it's a question in practice of deciding what not to put on them. Not this, it's too male. The sign says I'm out to meet an unplanned event. Please do not contact me with offers or services. For now my tribute remains this side of the virtual. I ran down the darkened passageway to receive my scar. I will never say this out loud.

Ohne Titel (Selbstporträt) 1975 by A.R. Penck. Grey & black ink wash on paper.
Presented to the British Museum by Count Christian Duerckheim.
© A.R. Penck/DACS 2013, courtesy of the Trustees of the British Museum.

THE GEOFFREY DEARMER PRIZE 2013

Judge: John Glenday

The winner of the Geoffrey Dearmer Prize is Mir Mahfuz Ali for 'MIG-21 Raids at Shegontola'. Paul Farley once commented that a great novel is a page-turner, but a great poem is a page stopper. When I was reading through the list of entries, I found myself going back to this poem again and again. There was something about it that caught my attention and held it.

It's always difficult choosing between the various strengths of different poems. Every effective poem works in a different way – each is a combination of craft, insight and imagination, but in Mir Mahfuz Ali's poem there is another ingredient – necessity. And by necessity I mean that quality which allows the poem to take a moral stance, to act as a redemptive force, rescuing the individual from history. In this respect, it is a form of first aid for the soul, telling the world in us a little more about the world out there.

The poem immediately draws us in to its heartbreaking narrative – as is always the case, big things need to be talked about in small ways. It begins with a small boy caught up in savagery, and ends with that same boy surviving, but transformed. He uses striking imagery to build a visceral description of the attack, juxtaposing images of violence and astonishing beauty. There are no fancy tricks nor virtuoso flauntings here, just a vivid, enthralling, brutal account of aggression and its consequences. But remarkably, one of those consequences is quietly positive: this child survives, only just survives – but emerges "like an apprentice baker" – a subtle reference to sustenance and compassion, to life continuing.

I'd also like to commend Liz Berry for her wonderful poem 'Scenes from *The Passion: The Evening*'.

John Glenday's first collection, The Apple Ghost, won a Scottish Arts Council Book Award and his second, Undark, was a Poetry Book Society Recommendation, as was his third, Grain.

MIR MAHFUZ ALI

MIG-21 Raids at Shegontola

Only this boy moves
between the runes of trees
on his tricycle
when an eagle swoops,
releases two arrows
from its silver wings and melts
away faster than lightning.
Then a loud whistle
and a bang like dry thunder.
In a blink the boy sees
his house roof sink.
Feels his ears ripped off.
The blast puffs up a fawn smoke
bigger than a mountain cloud.
The slow begonias rattle
their scarlet like confetti.
Metal slashes
the trees and ricochets.
Wires and pipes snap
at the roots, quiver.
The whirling smoke packed
with bricks and cement,
chicken feathers and nigella seeds.
When the cloud begins
to settle on the ground,
the boy makes out buckled iron rods.
White soot descends
and he finds himself dressed
like an apprentice baker.

First published in The Poetry Review, *103:4, Winter 2013.*

Bullet

A bullet sheared my voice away before I could flee
and I have been bargaining with him ever since
as if he was a relative planning a long stay.
He had reason to be here because I was a troublemaker,

vermin that smelled of subversive acts against the state.
If I opened my mouth the weather changed faster
than language in heat. Revolt is the first literature.
He has a country to run. He uses songs to slay the enemy.

*If I do not sing the venom into people I will come out
mangled*, he warned. Now he sits like a thorn between
my vocal chords, dictating how my tongue should dance
to those chants. But they mean nothing to me.

What dwells in my throat are words, heavy like imperfect stones
rattling to express the emptiness of my mouth, wanting
to speak, wanting to explain that I will stop painting the city
with fire in exchange for a fragment of my voice.

He has been living with me for so long that sometimes
I want my heart to beat like him. Maybe I trust him,
I am not kidding. My son needs an uncle. He can stay
as long as he does not land at my feet like a bullet.

Mir Mahfuz Ali *was born in Dhaka, Bangladesh. He studied at Essex University. He dances, acts, and has worked as a male model and a tandoori chef. He has given readings and performances at the Royal Opera House, Covent Garden, and other theatres in Britain and beyond. His poems have appeared in* The Poetry Review, London Magazine, Poetry London, Ambit *and* PN Review. *Mahfuz was shortlisted for the New Writing Ventures Awards 2007 and the Picador Poetry Prize 2010. His poetry has been published in the anthology* Ten: New Poets from Spread the Word *(Bloodaxe Books, 2010), edited by Bernardine Evaristo and Daljit Nagra. His debut collection* Midnight, Dhaka *was published by Seren in May 2014.*

The Geoffrey Dearmer Prize *is awarded annually to the best poem in* The Poetry Review *by a poet who had not, before the issue in which their work appeared, published a collection. It is funded through the generosity of the Dearmer family in honour of the poet Geoffrey Dearmer, who was a Poetry Society member.*

HOME AND AWAY

Paul Farley, Selected Poems, *Picador, £16.99*
ISBN 9781447220428
Harry Clifton, The Holding Centre: Selected Poems 1974-2004
Bloodaxe, £12, ISBN 9781852249717

reviewed by William Wootten

. . .

Kids with Quality Street wrappers, Keith Chegwin as Fleance, what happens when Liverpool disappears for a billionth of a second: these are the territories of nostalgia, the pub quiz and the whimsical conceit. Explored in Paul Farley's poems, however, they are also domains of violence, disillusionment and mortality. One Quality Street wrapper makes the child see a dog "flayed alive", another buries him in an "Empire of moss and long barrow" and shows him Eurydice. Remembering how Cheggers played Shakespeare recalls youth's wasted hours and a boy's wasted promise. Even a billionth of a second can make the poet feel his age.

Likewise, Farley can come across as a very matey sort of poet. The place names, brand names, cultural and pop cultural references in his poems are partly there to solicit an "oh I remember that!" from the reader, a realisation of just what you and Paul Farley have in common. Some of his poems even talk out of the page to "you". Yet, once he's won your confidence and complicity, he likes to implicate you in his crimes and make you take the rap. In 'Treacle', the stand-out poem from his 1998 debut *The Boy from the Chemist is Here to See You*, Farley gets "you" fondly opening up a tin of Tate and Lyle, before pouring it over "your" head and tarring and feathering "you" for the sins of empire and the sugar trade. In 'The Power' from 2012's *The Dark Film*, you and the poet imagine a seaside pier into being, flattering one another's powers of invention, before committing imaginary arson.

Farley's poems commonly explore and mimic different technologies and media: he will allude to Vermeer or Joseph Beuys and admire the view of Google Earth; in 'The Scarecrow Wears a Wire', he'll even set up a rural sound installation. But the greatest affinity a Farley poem has is with film. He will frame the world in terms of camera shots, admire the texture of celluloid itself, and he will check out the view from the auditorium. He is especially entranced by film's ability to stop, stretch or speed up time, or to put it into reverse. This is partly a matter of eye-catching camera tricks: a "dead sheep's seconds long journey to nothing / with maggots working like a ball of fire" ('The Lapse'); "pools come to the boil / then turn to glass as divers zip them shut" ('Nostalgie Concrete'). More profoundly, the use of camera work is allied to his interest in geographical, biological and temporal perspectives: from the vast sweep of 'The Ages' where "The trees lay down their seam of coal as thin / as hammered gold leaf all afternoon" to the slowed panorama round the football ground and its environs in 'A Minute's Silence'.

The *Selected Poems* digs deep, but its range is not especially wide. Most poems fall into a few types and explore similar themes, strategies and tropes. Pentameters dominate heavily. These, admittedly, are of different varieties, come unrhymed, half-rhymed and rhymed, and can be arranged in some complex stanzas, but they are fairly uniform in feel and, with the few poems in short lines less sure of ear, their mastery seems to have been bought somewhat at the expense of broader technical virtuosity. Still, there are exceptions to prove the rule. The nicely shaped mixed metre stanzas of 'Civic' successfully essay a longer more disquisitional manner, and make clear Farley is not simply a narrow – if impressive – lyric talent. Indeed, when considered with the other long poem in this volume, 'Requiem for a Friend', it suggests that if he is to develop, it could well be as a writer of longer pieces.

Harry Clifton's poems may not have Farley's spectacle and punch – they tend to be quiet growers which improve on repeat reading – but they deploy a commendable range of lines and forms, free and metred verse, and can be particularly adept at playing speech cadence across rhyme and lyric line. What's more, Clifton is a poet whose work has changed, developed and improved considerably over the years.

The end date of *The Holding Centre: Selected Poems 1974-2004* is significant, for it is the year Clifton returned to Ireland after decades of living and working abroad: in Africa, Asia and in mainland Europe. One consequence of living away from home is that, rather than emphasising the familiar, Clifton draws attention to the strange and the estranged. Thus when 'Strawberry Fields Forever' plays in 'Government Quarters', it is described as "Defunct McCartney and Lennon / Circa 1967", less to aid the ignorant than to unsettle those who recognise its words, flipping round the customary order of the writing partnership, and underlining how, now and in Africa, it is out of place and time, switched on by the "government electricity / Our memory units work by". The situation is somewhat similar with the title of Clifton's book. It may allude to "the centre cannot hold" from W.B. Yeats's 'The Second Coming', yet its primary reference, a Holding Centre in Thailand in 1981, a "prison that saves", is far from anything anticipated by Yeats's poem.

Clifton seeks to resist as well as to register estrangement and dislocation, to find ethical, political and spiritual bearings among the people and places he describes. These can be over-conspicuous. Telling us that 'The Seamstress' "Where women are still slaves... sews the garment of pure freedom I have asked for" spells out a moral we could have reasonably been left to figure for ourselves. They can also, perhaps, not be quite conspicuous enough. The clichés of race and eroticism in 'Monsoon Girl' ("Chinese women, / Blank and inscrutable"; "I feed on the lotus-flower / Of your delicate sex") may well be intended subtly to betray the frame of mind of a Westerner visiting a Chinese prostitute in Bangkok, but it isn't clear that they aren't just clichés.

'Death of Thomas Merton', from Clifton's 1982 volume *Comparative Lives*, manages to address the political, cultural and spiritual concerns confronting a Westerner in Asia through the depiction of the end of the American monk, mystic, writer and social activist. In so doing, it points the way to the more controlled and accomplished later poems. Indeed, Clifton is often his best when escaping his own self and identity more or less entirely, being 'The Poet Sandro Penna, in Old Age', or viewing nineteenth-century Russia from the perspective of 'The Nihilists'. Still, reading about 'Attila József's Trains', 'MacNeice's London', rather than Clifton's own, and with even his Dublin mediated by James Joyce, the experience and imagination does feel second hand. So it is refreshing to read 'Søren Kierkegaard', a poem about a nine-hour train journey spent *not* reading Kierkegaard.

If calling the later Clifton post-modernist suggests an Irish Ashbery, it's not the term to use – John Ashbery he isn't. But Clifton is often exploring what it is to be very nearly post-something, and that includes post-Irish. In 'Cloudberry' the search for Irishness becomes at one with the search to transcend it, with its wish "to go back" "behind all that is Ireland, / To the age of free migrations / Where a man sets out, with only a Word in his head" and to "eat of the tasteless fruit / Of universality, rooted / Like myself, in the invisible, / And belonging everywhere."

This is more nearly post-nation and post-modern than it is post-Christian. Although Clifton is not exactly a religious poet, throughout *The Holding Centre* he is much preoccupied by the Church and its servants, and with Western and Eastern religion and spirituality. He mixes sacred and profane love, as in 'Early Christians'. Breaking from his usual style and personae to write the religious allegories 'Firefly' and 'The River', he makes for an effective mystical poet. In the later, European, poems, the depiction of religion becomes more playful: we witness the God of 'Friesian Herds', and we even find 'God in France' sampling its human delights. But a poet who celebrates the sensuous secular state from the viewpoint of God probably isn't quite over religion just yet. The centre may not have held, but significant parts of it may be found at the periphery.

William Wootten's reviews and poems have appeared widely. He teaches at Bristol University.

HOSPITAL BEDS

John Burnside, All One Breath, *Cape, £10*
ISBN 9780224097406
Hugo Williams, I Knew the Bride, *Faber, £12.99*
ISBN 9780571308880

reviewed by Aingeal Clare

. . .

John Burnside is among the most mysterious of contemporary poets, with enough ghosts and animal spirits flitting round most of his books to keep any séance or taxidermist busy. But where so much darkness might slow some poets down, the pace of the average Burnside poem is anything but funereal. On the contrary, he barges through his poems with a positively athletic turn of pace. Burnside has always been fond of breaking lines across adjective-noun combinations, and in the first poem alone of *All One Breath*, his thirteenth collection, we find a "rose-print / sundress", an "off-white / fabric", a "baby-faced / pariah", a "little / criminal", "male / homunculus", and "the life / perpetual". These are, as the title suggests, poems to be read all in one breath.

Also in an almighty rush are the spirits of the departed, who traverse the ether as though in a vast Hadron collider. In 'The Wake', we read of bereaved daughters covering mirrors that might have "kept [their mother] from the afterlife" and the threat of the ghost "coming home untransformed", because "whatever happens in the life to come, / you'd hardly want to drag the self along". This unquestioned tilting of the scales in favour of the unself becomes a problem in the long run, for the sceptical reader. The intrinsic interest of the ghost over the person is so much an article of faith as to need no demonstration, even when it means little more in practice than a series of poltergeist movie tricks – thumbprints on a cup, haunted mirrors, noises in an empty room. This assumes comic proportions in 'A Rival', which begins with the poet daydreaming of a fantasy woman, who then begins to make eyes at his partner, "because it's clear she'd rather you than me". Well, you started it.

Occasionally Burnside's spiritualism acquires a Christian tinge, or more correctly a wan afterglow of late Eliot, burnishing the Scottish poet's credentials as one of the "residual beneficiaries" of literary Anglicanism invoked by Geoffrey Hill. It is slightly too revealing of Burnside, in 'A Couple', to talk of "a practised, *unheimlich* manoeuvre". Amusing though it is to picture the poet performing a first-aid procedure on a ghost, the whole point about the *unheimlich* is that it cannot be practised and must remain a small miracle of surprise: anything else and we have entered the dread territory of the Parnassian. For all these reasons, and their higgledy-piggledy line-breaks notwithstanding, poems that permit themselves the solidity, the weight of the merely actual, such as 'My Grandmother, Elizabeth Burnside, 1962', 'On the Vanishing of My Sister, Aged 3, 1965', and 'Tommy McGhee, Corby Works, 1981', speak with a conviction and authority far in excess of Burnside's wispier things. It is here, rather than in self-haunting retreads of his last few collections, that Burnside's future most profitably lies. If only more of *All One Breath* were like this, to paraphrase Dr Johnson, it had been vain to blame and useless to praise it.

Over-ambitious excursions in the astral sphere have never been a problem for Hugo Williams. In 'Eucalyptus' we find him opening his wallet (twice) to look at his "list of excuses" – ever the reluctant lead in his own drama – and nervously sneaking a peek at his lines. As it happens, he does experience an out-of-body experience later in the same poem, but this is more momentary light-headedness than anything cosmic. Like Mae West, Williams does a high proportion of his best work in bed. In his anthology piece 'Poetry', sex is immediately followed by a worry about where to put the line-breaks in the poem that will follow, and in 'Rhyming' here the poet lies in wait for a lover "on the blank sheet of the bed / while you drift about the room / improvising on a theme". When Burnside indulges in this kind of self-displacement it is the *unheimlich*, but when Williams does it, it is whimsy. If the man at the other side of the bar "must me be", calling home to say "I'm going to be late", the effect is reassuring, with an understanding of the pleasantly distorting effects of camaraderie and romance, still regnant passions in the Williams *oeuvre* almost a half-century after his début.

Post-coital anxieties about literary form return in 'Twenty Yards Behind', a rare Williams attempt at a strict form (the villanelle) that sees him rhyme "nonsense" with "detumescence". It's not the most successful poem in the book, with the detumescent effect of male disappointment spelled out too heavily on the page, instead of being sent on its way with a signature airy quip (and what a cruelly flaccid word "detumescence" is). Questions of weight versus airiness return in 'Falling', which recycles a too-familiar cliché about falling being okay – it's coming to a stop on the ground that's the problem.

Williams's elegies for his sister and a sequence of poems on his treatment for kidney failure offer more rewarding opportunities for the cheerfulness at all the wrong moments that shows him at his best (the second half of *I Knew the Bride* is noticeably stronger than the first). Life is a hospital where all the patients want to change beds, Baudelaire said, and in these poems about illness Williams shows the steel behind the whimsy in meditations on the arbitrariness of suffering and death. "I'd have to recommend dialysis / to anyone looking for a break / from their daily routine", begins one, while by the end of the dialysis sequence the weary speaker remembers being alive "as if it were yesterday".

At such moments Williams's work goes beyond the easy fluency and charm for which it is singled out by its admirers and detractors alike. "Strange how potent cheap music is", said Noël Coward, and in his best poems, rather than choose between them, Williams splices high and low, the tasteful and the flippant, the heartfelt and the throwaway. Modern poetry has a long history of writers who win popular readerships on the basis of their apparent charm, beneath whose surface something darker and more disturbing lurks, and Lionel Trilling caused all manner of offence when he pointed out what a "terrifying" rather than reassuring poet Robert Frost was. Williams will not be turning into Geoffrey Hill any day soon, but the laughs in *I Knew the Bride* give us a sharper sense than previously in this poet's work of the skull beneath the skin. Since I've now mentioned splicing opposites, I should end with a call for John Burnside's next book to be a series of showbiz anecdotes and Hugo Williams's to be a Heideggerian study of selkie myths from the Fife coast. While that might be a case too far of Baudelaire's musical chairs, or hospital beds, the point stands: the most interesting things about both books under review here go against the grain of what we know, or think we know, about their authors. In their different ways, and with varying degrees of success, these two books remind us that the real challenge for poets is to surprise not just their readers but themselves.

Aingeal Clare has written for the Guardian, TLS *and* London Review of Books.

ACTS OF ATTENTION

Tiffany Atkinson, So Many Moving Parts, *Bloodaxe, £9.95*
ISBN 9781852249526
Thomas A. Clark, Yellow & Blue, *Carcanet. £9.95*
ISBN 9781847772053
Vona Groarke, X, *Gallery, €11.95*
ISBN 9781852355760

reviewed by Julia Bird

. . .

Are you reading this by the pool? Is this Summer issue of *The Poetry Review* part of your holiday reading? Add to that book pile Tiffany Atkinson's third collection. At its heart is a little run of five beach-based poems, unannounced as a sequence, but functioning together as a single area of enquiry. The poet sits in the shade of the windbreak, looking out onto sunlit activity. "There's / a knack that women all over the world have / of putting up hair in a knot, the pale nape gathers / the salt", she observes of the paddlers in 'Beachcombing' on her way to the unwelcome realisation that "I have spent a half-life / on the wrong strand". Meanwhile, the 'Woman with Paperback Romance' "snorts at each / flipped page" while "young men detonate / across the baked sand" even as she counts down the days till the end of her holiday and a return to "rush-hour, shopping, heartache". In the way that holidays never really distract us from our day-to-day affairs but rather illuminate them with differently angled sunshine, Atkinson's beach is a place for her to examine the enterprises common to her whole collection, but one where the light is fiercer and the available camouflage less merciful than usual. The 'Girl with Blue Towel', barely aware of the effect her skimpy, stripy bikini has on the hotel's resident photographer, represents an early stage of the life cycle experienced a step later by the narrator of 'The Starling Cloud'. Here, the poet, now inland of the beach, is baffled and excluded by the joy of Gruff and Harry on the climbing frame in the beer garden of a family pub: "Who put them there? ... how did I exempt myself?" A step further, and we're with 'Havisham': "By then I'd used so little of myself / my voice was cracked, my muscles / dragged, my breasts had crawled // inside my chest". The friction between action and observation energises Atkinson's poems to release confident, sometimes uncomfortable, truths about balancing the longing to team up with the desire for solitude. The wide-ranging tones and registers of these poems will stay with you much longer than your holiday tan.

Solitude whistles through Thomas A. Clark's *Yellow & Blue*. The first of the book's two hundred or so untitled, un-numbered, unpunctuated poems reads in its entirety:

> on a morning early
> when no one
> is around
> the scree slope
> tumbles into
> the green lochan

It begins an extraordinary series of tiny acts of attention to the natural world, each of which is part haiku, part photo. Clark walks through the Highlands and Islands of Scotland with the focus of a nature diarist, isolating the smallest elements of the sublime and scenic – "the peeling / birch bark", "the mountain pansy" which "is blue and yellow / briefly", "grey screes", "black leeches" – to create poetry of the wild in the calmest, most meditative of styles. These landscapes are not the setting for action, they are themselves the action. Sometimes laid out three to a page, they are spare as an act of erasure performed on an Alice Oswald collection, but they are richly concentrated and cumulative in their power. Human encounters are rare:

the residue
of the dissolution
of being
together
huddles
in desolation
by a lonely shore

The hissing, shushing language of this particular example hides its figures in a mist. If nature could write its own poems without the need of any human intervention, perhaps they would look like this.

Clark is an artist as well as a poet, and his poems and texts have often been installed in landscapes, galleries and interiors. It would be interesting to experience these latest poems stencilled on a wall or carved into the landscape, separated by space and therefore time. It's a disciplined reader indeed who can obey this paperback's white-space instruction to slow down so each flicker and fragment can receive its due consideration. To read these pages too quickly is to take a speed-yoga class: your muscles will get a stretch, but your soul won't. A friend of mine once had a box of Bible verses on minute scrolls to be tweezed out one at a time for contemplative purposes. Take Clark's poems at a similar pace, the better to pray upon them.

Picking which path to follow through Vona Groarke's collection as signposted by its title could confound a reader prone to choice paralysis. Should we be looking for kisses, votes, negations? Times tables, illiterate signatures or buried treasure? Start perhaps with 'ex', and the section of poems which begins the book. 'A White Year' searches for enlightenment in "the museum / of the everyday" in which "no dust whatsoever // is to be found on the bedside chair, / unopened perfume, / impeccable gold quilt". In France an *année blanche* is a year that's wasted. In the poem, there's the sense of a past trial whose aftermath still troubles: "There is before and after / surely, and there is discretion // to be accounted for, and grief". Whatever has happened, the dust has surely not settled. In 'X', the poem which follows, X is the intersection of "brushstroked husband / and brushstroked wife" but also "the blades of a bedroom ceiling fan / come to // a perfectly oblivious stop" – a painful image of the marital mechanism winding down. If Thomas A. Clark's bell-clear nature notes elicit sympathetically resonating moods in the reader, Groarke's poems are scores of the moods themselves. The concatenated images she lays over a complex syntax (twenty-one lines without a full-stop in 'X') are not brightly coloured Ladybird book illustrations of her concerns. She doesn't look to describe neat sensational equivalencies, but builds up a mosaic of associations and impressions which results in a direct transference of emotion from writer to reader.

'The White Garden' is one of thirteen poems in 'The Garden Sequence'. In it is planted the moon, a white poppy and a "table top / of Carrara marble". Although all thirteen gardens ('The New Garden', 'The Blue Garden', 'The Garden as an Island Approached by a Tidal Causeway', et al) are not mere settings for a new hobby to distract from painful situations, they are sites of self-examination and renewal. "Come the rain", "come the wind", "come morning" the poem proceeds, suggesting both the fatalistic acceptance of whatever the future holds and an invitation to a fight. In this case, as throughout this disquieting, affecting collection, X equals multiple values.

Julia Bird's most recent collection is Twenty-four Seven Blossom *(Salt Publishing, 2013).*

LANDS OF SPICE

Kathryn Simmonds, The Visitations, *Seren, £8.99*
ISBN 9781781721162
Kevin Powers, Letter Composed During a Lull in the Fighting
Sceptre, £12.99, ISBN 9781444780819

reviewed by Julian Stannard

. . .

T*he Visitations* is a collection of beautifully made poems invigorated by a special kind of wit. As the title suggests, they are mindful of the sacred. But there's nothing pious or holier-than-thou about any of them; these are poems which light candles in a quiet side chapel rather than going in for showy theatrics. The titles themselves – 'Sunday Morning', 'On the Island of San Michele', 'Madonna of the Pomegranate', 'In a Church', 'Apocryphal', 'Forgiveness', not to mention the title poem – offer up their own special liturgy. Although Julian of Norwich plays a cameo role in 'Hermits', the pursuit of the numinous is enhanced here by means of secular strategy. In 'Sunday Morning' the church bells are comfortably in the distance and there's no beating a path to the church door: "Since I've stopped praying", we are told, "I've got so much more done", and "Since I've stopped considering the nature / of the soul, the infinite, all that, / I've found the joy of gardening". But this isn't a true recantation because, although the speaker is eating chocolates in bed and "the words of the psalms [are] dissolving like an old dream", she has an awareness that "He'll find me, if he chooses".

Poems as prayer make one think of George Herbert's sumptuous rendering: "Church-bells beyond the stars heard, the soul's blood, / The land of spices, something understood". Simmonds might hold onto a shard of mystery or – as in 'The Visitations' – spin out knowingly mischievous rhymes:

Sometimes God comes as a tiger,
And sometimes as a rose –
He opens for you secretly,
Perfuming your nose.

[...]

Sometimes he comes as sunlight –
Watch him tick across the wall.
And sometimes as a boxing glove.
And sometimes not at all.

Or she might, at times, fashion a response to Larkin's question "What are days for?" Part of the answer to that lies in getting on and getting through ("Days are where we live"). In 'Self-Portrait with Washing-up Glove' the irritations and banalities of the day are duly catalogued: "As I remove the freezer shelf, my neighbour / hollers at her child. A scattering of frozen peas / are stuck to something pink." And even if the higher power is invoked he seems as unhelpful as an absentee landlord: "Oh God, we should amend our lives, / all of us who sleep in rented beds" and "all of us who've lived our best days / in the imagination's potting shed."

Larkin answers the question by bringing in the doctor and the priest, and both these roles are taken on in *The Visitations* by the therapist and the life coach. The middle section of the book (the most formulaic) is called 'Life Coach Variations'. Even here there are some wonderfully ungodly moments. In 'The Life Coach on the Stairs' our modern hero finds himself "Halfway up, or down", forgetting "entirely what prompted this". In fact, "He might hover all afternoon, / become an African, / a woman, a tomato plant. What was it? / Are these even his feet?"

Or perhaps the workshop is the new evangelism. 'What I Did in My

Summer Holidays' is a droll demonstration of creative writing doctrine (which might, in fact, have us think of Billy Collins's 'Workshop'). In effect, Simmonds's dexterity, comic-seriousness, assuredness of touch in this excellent collection, are amply demonstrated in the 'sacramental' space where poets nowadays spend half their lives: "We talked / last week about the stanza, you might think of stanzas as little / rooms: what are you going to do in yours? Are you going to just / lie there watching light reinvent itself?" Or (indeed) "Did anyone else have a problem with the turnip metaphor?"

By comparison, in some ways, Kevin Powers's *Letter Composed During a Lull in the Fighting* is a difficult book to review. He is a young war veteran who fought in Iraq and is the author of the widely acclaimed novel *The Yellow Birds*. He is a soldier-poet whose experiences put him beyond almost anyone who is a non-combatant, and which therefore places the literary critic in a somewhat invidious position. Consider 'Separation', whose title reminds us of the inevitable disconnect between soldiers and non-soldiers, and which also reminds us of those Vietnam films where the returning soldier is either lifted onto a pedestal, or is seen as the unwanted custodian of the nation's dark (collective) conscience:

> I want the boys at the end of the bar
> to know, these young Republicans
> in pink popped-collar shirts, to know
> that laughter drives me mad
>
> [...]
>
> I want to rub their clean
> bodies in blood. I want my rifle
>
> [...]
> I felt
> so old: twenty-four and crying
> for my rifle and the boys
> at the end of the bar
> were laughing.

How does one walk into hell, limp out and find a way of writing about it? In 'Meditation on a Main Supply Route ', we are told "I am home, and whole, so to speak" and that qualification points to the trauma happening off the battlefield and which is central to the collection. In the centenary of the Great War soldier-poets occupy a special place. There is no lack of media attention regarding geo-political conflict. But we turn to the soldier-poet for a different kind of witness. Powers has served his time, too, in the classroom (an MFA from the University of Texas) and is therefore no naive recorder of experience. His poetic instincts are recognisably American: lines of varying length, the conversational voice, at moments a meandering accumulation of information before striking the emphatic note, as if he were a fisherman casting the line. One might demur at occasional philosophical flights, as if he were straying from the Williams-ite dictum he generally holds onto – "No ideas but in things". He can be 'confessional' (even Lowellian) – see 'After Leaving McGuire Veterans' Hospital for the Last Time' – and he can take a sideways look: home, history, theatre(s) of war, memory, dream, ensure that borders, both psychological and geographical, are skilfully negotiated. In 'While Trying to Make an Arrowhead in the Fashion of the Mattaponi Indians', he says "We are born to be makers of crude tools. / And our speech is full of cruel / signifiers: you, me, them, us. I / am sure we will not survive." If a poem is itself a kind of bullet, there's no lack of force in the title poem:

> I tell her in a letter that will stink,
> when she opens it,
> of bolt oil and burned powder
> and the things it says.
>
> I tell her how Private Bartle says, offhand,
> that war is just us
> making little pieces of metal
> pass through each other.

Julian Stannard's The Street of Perfect Love *will be published by Worple Press later this year.*

NOSTALGIA WITH FRILLS

Rory Waterman, Tonight the Summer's Over, *Carcanet, £9.95*
ISBN 9781847772077
Selima Hill, The Sparkling Jewel of Naturism, *Bloodaxe, £9.95*
ISBN 9781780371030
Amy Key, Luxe, *Salt, £9.99*
ISBN 9781844719716

reviewed by Katherine Angel

. . .

The title of Rory Waterman's collection, *Tonight the Summer's Over*, announces an acute awareness of the trickling away of time, of the past already in the present. In the opening poem, 'Navigating' (pursuing a heron, not knowing what comes after the next river bend), Waterman seeks to understand, retrospectively, the joy of being in the present – and throughout the collection, to understand that which has slipped away, and from which some insight, solace or regret can be wrought.

'Retrospect' encapsulates what is both most and least satisfying in Waterman's writing. Seeing an owl hit by a train – "Pristine, unbloodied, slightly flat" – he describes the world (often the natural world) with an acuity verging on a pleasing insolence ("You fan a wing / which springs half back towards its holding"). The poem addresses the impossibility of truly understanding, in the moment, what we are encountering: "at thirteen you don't think it's anything / you won't see the same way again // like toys, cartoons, just months ago". Waterman looks back at this scene, understanding now what he didn't realise was there to be understood at the time. But he doesn't trust his readers – or perhaps himself – enough, and wants to tell us what we should glean from it: "Four frail claws curl / in your cruel hand – you're holding hands / with a wise dead owl, and learning something / inscrutable you still can't understand". The delicate tension between temporal modes is, I'd suggest, undermined.

Retrospect, in fact, dominates the collection. In 'An Email from your Mother', "Home will never, quite, be waiting / the way it was; your childhood is receding / too far". Again, Waterman extracts the core idea a little too forcefully: "Is growing older, then, forced unclenching?" He is clearly interested in compressing observations into specific formal structures – which might enable his tendency to push a thought to its logical, but not always necessary, conclusion; structures are there to be written into, to sometimes problematic effect. This quatrain's force is diluted in the last two lines, and it is in poems' endings that Waterman sometimes veers into a disappointing one-toneness. Freer structures might free him from some rather thudding last lines; he might stop sooner, and more powerfully.

The more present-saturated, almost photographic poems are the most successful. Indeed, 'Faroe Islands: Notes for Three Photographs' is my favourite. The first, about arctic terns that "head-butt spume / then flick away, beak-heavy / in lithe, bounding vs", has a pleasing sharpness of observation. The second, on eating puffins, moved me and also made me laugh: "I sucked each tiny bone, left / a splat-doused tablecloth, felt / a bit more interesting". The third teeters into the realm of Waterman I like least: the urge to spell out a preoccupation with ageing and time, and to pronounce – the last line sees him pushing "at death with my boots". But there is real skill here – a gracious precision in capturing a texture and conveying, rather than stating, something important. The same is true of the high-resolution 'Reverdie', in which "a bee revs its engine / and limps from stamen / to stamen", and of 'The Lake', a short, violent evocation of brutality (a girl's dead body: somebody had "flopped her in the silt / with care"), whose musicality stands in a rich relationship to its subject matter. The more aggressive, terse and indeed playful Waterman gets – in 'You're a shower of bastards', about language itself, with its "randiness of rabbits, a shit of sheep", and 'Note to Self: Chip Shop Battered Sausage and Other Meat' – the less ponderous, more agile and more impressive he is.

Toddlers feature in several of Waterman's poems, and children are central in Selima Hill's *The Sparkling Jewel of Naturism*. The collection opens bluntly in the moment – "To me, I'm me. To you, I'm someone fabulous / someone you're so jealous of it hurts" – with a narrator speaking to and of a sister. This relationship is a bind, a link that can't be broken, suffused with resentment and anger. A mercilessness lurks in this 'Doormat' series. Later, the 'Happiness is Just a Waste of Time' series conjures a magical, sinister and unsettling world of young girls. Hill writes from a precarious place between the first and third person, and evokes both the strangeness of children and of how adults perceive them. In some poems – most are very brief, two stanzas of two lines each – she is the little girl ("At meal-times / we kick our skinny legs"); in others she pronounces on the girl ("Little girls should wait – like little car parks / that don't know what it is they should be waiting for"). The latter formulation might also be the little girl speaking – as spoken by Hill, of course – and connotes both a well-worn injunction about girlhood (little girls should...), and its acerbic, feminist parody. The tone hovers uncomfortably between these two, perhaps intentionally.

In moments, Hill's evocations veer dangerously close to the mawkish. As with Waterman's 'Unfolding', with its childlike flat, continuous syntax (you "wrote your name on it // and Mummy said that she thought it was very good / and stuck it on the fridge with Blu-tack"), Hill can lurch into the chintzy cuteness, the earnest lispiness that can beset writing about children – as in 'Shampoo', or 'Polystyrene': "If little girls / were made of polystyrene // they'd be less pink / but even squeakier".

Hill is powerful, though, on the ambivalent appeal of youth, on its contrast to our curdled adulthood, and its dangerous ability to lure in the jaded. The sinister projection upon children, the urge to be or to have what they are – smoothness, intensity, uncompromisingness – ripples through 'Trout' and 'Crocodiles'. In the latter, Hill evokes youth's incipient deathliness, with crocodiles "that lurk in nurseries in the roots of mangrove swamps // crunching dentures, watches, hats and body parts". There's a macabre element to this series, a Paul Delvaux-like landscape of skeletons, rot and beauty, drawing out the fear of death which suffuses the act of looking back at youth. The 'Fly of My Youth' "spends its day at work on rump and tail / bows to no one, will not be my pet".

Hill's girls are resignedly aware of what their girlhood means. Amy Key does something different with girlhood – or young womanhood – in *Luxe*.

The paraphernalia and accoutrements of femininity clutter this collection. Highly saturated with the present, *Luxe* captures a cascade of surfaces, smells and colours as they tumble in and out of view. In the opening poem, 'Brand New Lover', "I'm all texture. Silk rosette, billowing coral / tentative as a just baked cake"; "My mouth is a glass paperweight / to keep our tastes in". It ends with a stanza of assured intensity: "This is not about a future / with a decorative child. Layer your pulse / onto my pulse. Dress me."

Key is freer with form than Waterman – there are more idiosyncratic structures here – but her contained rhythmic sensibility yields some powerful phrases, as in '"Too Gruesome!"': "She wept. Faux-wept. Wept." Many poems have a subtle, controlled eroticism; in 'Highlights in the History of Concrete', "I pout / angles and slopes, after all, I want her to lie down on me. / To be her pavilion". In 'Pretty Please': "At night I prefer you lax", and "I want to not know / what to do". Lines land with a narcotic surety and fullness. It's a skill, however, of which Key isn't always in control. 'To a Clothes Rail' ("Cocktail-drinking dress, unsittable-down-in / Dress best worn with a brutalist pendant") is an incantation that's as melancholy as it is charming, but has a slackness that occasionally disappoints, as in '"Too Gruesome!"' ("I wish ironed pillowcases counted for something, / though I've learned kindnesses don't").

Key's elaborate, glittering spaces are ones in which she fantasises and luxuriates, but also in which she teases apart connotations of femininity. In 'Transmitting the Fatigue of the Painter', "a dress cannot save you":

> no dress   will make   a dolly of you.

In 'Her', Key plays with the idea of women's bodies as constrained consumables: "I think of her starlet lit, / of her mouth, sealed by peach skin. Of her preserved / in glue, her patent red hair, the faux fruit of her". She rolls around with glee in well-worn associations of femininity with artifice and construction, while also fixing a keen eye on femininity's calibration. In 'Yes, She Seemed Demure', "I so keenly wanted to know her, / but she was unwearable to me – shiny harp-string hair, / the way her throat buttoned-up to mute – with my overt / everythings. One night I went home / to unfloozy myself".

Overtness and flooziness can be put on and taken off, yet Key refuses to cast glamour as the enemy. *Luxe* is overwhelmed with sugary ornament – fake yellow roses, tender-stemmed glassware, bubbles, sorbet – in an accumulation of objects that is near-suffocating. But objects, and sensual relationships with them, are vehicles of thought and feeling; they bear a great weight. Key may occasionally veer close to cliché in the teetering significance she gives them – "Wrote I'm sorry in white petals" in 'But a Love Poem Will not Fail' – but there is a deliberate sumptuousness here, at times nostalgic and retro, as in 'Some Day We Must Come Back and Explore Properly', with its "Coke floats" and "custard candyfloss hair". Key takes seriously that which often gets dismissed as the frilly froth of femininity. She gives plenitude to what is cast as fragile, forgettable, contemptible. There's gravity, moreover, to taking the world of fragile things seriously: glass, dust and ornaments conjure evanescence and decay as much as frivolity or joy. Key is a poet refusing to dismiss the seriousness, fullness, and depths of surface, glamour, glitz.

Katherine Angel is the author of Unmastered: A Book on Desire, Most Difficult to Tell *(Penguin, 2012).*

OF HEARTH AND HEART

Jen Hadfield, Byssus, *Picador, £9.99*
ISBN 9781447241102
Lavinia Greenlaw, A Double Sorrow: Troilus and Criseyde
Faber, £16.99
ISBN 9780571284542

reviewed by Sandeep Parmar

. . .

The core of Jen Hadfield's *Byssus* is poetic strangeness or, rather, the circularity of language, which names no thing wholly but itself. The natural and human worlds, and the living archive of Shetland dialect, detach and abut uncomfortably around those things that definitions cannot with any singular authority *place*. Hadfield's lyric voice is very much the poet's, and her revelry in linguistic possibility is born of an alien landscape (or so it feels to the uninitiated reader and perhaps, at times, to Hadfield herself, who is a non-native Shetlander). The epigraph to 'In Memoriam', from Iain Crichton Smith's poem 'On Looking at the Dead', "No metaphors swarm / around that fact... that being that was and now no longer is", oddly marks out the liminal spaces of abstract nouns that Hadfield's work inhabits; the most abstract of all – death – is "This unspeakable is not *like* / anything". Where "language abdicates" it is the poet's responsibility to rediscover the newness that invigorates a linguistic relationship between the self and the landscape. And there is much local terrain here, reminded as we are of its unfamiliarity by a glossary of 'Shetland Words'. Hadfield's work is at its strongest where the annunciation of this strangeness takes language down to its foundations, effaces the poet and is the least personal, as in the book's opening poem 'Lichen', and 'The Black Hole':

> A ring of down-feathers surrounds the corpse
> of the blackbird, thickly leaved like pages
> of a burnt book. The cat steels himself at
> their stirring perimeter. I've seen him
> biff a robin's carcass to make it look
> lively [...]

This is a conversation with the self that is as much about the poet's inheritance of description ("like pages of a burnt book") as it is about residual, accompanying silences: "who listens / like lichen listens" ('Lichen'). These images are sharp, deft and rarely fail to startle with their verbal reserve: "prunk", "biff", "gape" have precise visual energy. Hadfield's poems are both about mushrooms ('Ceps', 'The Puffballs' and also 'Puffballs') and mushroom-like (both uncultivated and unexpected); the walker forages for them as the poet forages for the covert (possibly toxic?) pleasures of words:

> To snack on you – sheepish – where you grow
> is like eating *löragub*, sea-haze, expanding foam.
>
> To sniff your socket in the grass
> is to recall some humid porch of the body.
>
> [...]
>
> and you live
> to sing to blurt
>
> your spore-mass
> from your ragged
>
> moue!

('Puffballs')

'Ceps', a porcini-like fungus, reasserts the book's implied relationship between language, loss and discovery. Described as a moon-like terrain of "ice-shattered rock, riddled / with arctic scramblers", the dramatic Shetland coastland delivers up the unique mushroom as if it were a warning:

> this mushroom, like a piece
> of vernacular furniture,
> tough droiltin tree
> that seems to sprout
> from the language of heart
> and hearth; massy corbel
> of the least willow [...]

In *Byssus*, Hadfield's "vernacular furniture" is intentionally displaced from its familiar hearth. Where the book disappoints is in the more conventional lyrics – which the acknowledgements suggest are commissions or occasional challenges that seem merely to have expended their impetus without becoming powerfully generative acts – like 'The White Goods' and the banally-titled 'We climb the hill in the dark and the children are finally given back their iPhones'. But there is laudable innovation here: Hadfield's use of the page, of its potential space and its visual-linguistic cues, is often liberating.

As Lavinia Greenlaw points out in her introduction to *A Double Sorrow: Troilus and Criseyde*, "the seeds of war, like those of tragedy, are usually a series of consequences". From Homer's *Iliad* we know the story of Troy's ten-year siege and are at least acquainted with the figure of Troilus as a Trojan prince murdered by Achilles. It is not until the medieval period, however, that through a variety of sources ranging from the twelfth-century French poet Benoît de Sainte-Maure to Boccaccio's fourteenth-century *Il Filostrato*, we arrive at Chaucer's definitive version of the 'love story' of *Troilus and Criseyde*. Its heroine is an odd invention who, it would seem, exists to fulfil the narrative demands of courtly love and in this she takes her place next to Helen as the second most faithless woman in an oft-retold mythical tragedy. Briefly, the series of consequences (as told by Chaucer) is thus: Troilus, son of King Priam and brother to Paris and Hector, falls in love with Criseyde, the abandoned daughter of the prophet Calchas, who has himself escaped to the Greek encampment foreseeing that Troy will fall. Widowed but beautiful, Criseyde is convinced by her uncle Pandarus to form a romantic liaison with the Trojan prince. Soon after, an exchange of prisoners between armies means that Criseyde is given over to the Myrmidons and returned to her father's care. Troilus is distraught. Criseyde swears to return but, realising it is impossible to keep her promise, makes the best of her situation and aligns herself with the Greek warrior Diomede. Troilus is finally put out of his misery by Achilles.

Greenlaw is keen to convince us that her book is not a version of Chaucer or of Boccaccio's version of the Matter of Troy (itself an accumulation of versions). Rather, her book is an "extrapolation" that builds on images and elaborates on phrases from both medieval texts. Line numbers indicate from where, precisely, the poet is extrapolating and subtitles act "as a form of detonation". Greenlaw's project concerns itself with form: she takes Chaucer's rime royal (seven-line stanza rhymed ABABBCC) and makes a convincing argument for its unfinished and inconclusive quality in a story that never stops retelling itself. As Chaucer borrowed heavily from previous versions, Greenlaw's retelling relies on a near-chronological ritual dance (in aptly prefigured steps) through Chaucer's poem – and as the reader follows Greenlaw's text (and sees Chaucer's and Boccaccio's line numbers) she cannot but compare each section painstakingly with its predecessors. Inevitably, there are moments when the fluidity of Chaucer's rich language cannot be matched – and although, at times, a valid and unexplored angle is hit upon by Greenlaw's commentary, one struggles to see always the real contribution to an already familiar narrative. The extrapolation stops short of invention. Elsewhere, the poet fruitfully builds on what she herself refers to as "irrevocable step[s]... aspects of the compacted emotion... decisions, gestures..." What, for example, is Pandarus's role and what are his motives?

> A man who wanders the corridors
> Who presses his ear to the wall
> Who rushes in as if to the rescue.
> Has the prince – flat out, sobbing – been hurt
> Or has some devilry borne fruit?
> He pulls up in a chair.
> He can taste the juice.
>
> ('Pandarus')

Chaucer's description of Pandarus's entrance into Troilus's tale of woe is oddly vague: "a freend of his, that was called Pandare, / Com ones in unwar, and herde him grone" (*I.* 548-9). Greenlaw rightly hones in on Pandarus's duplicity (he is also Criseyde's uncle) and his pandering to Troilus's desires – who is this interloper who "wanders corridors"? Her descriptions of Criseyde early in the book display a fitting intensity of language and a satisfyingly ironic intertextual distance from the plot:

> In her presence we know ourselves most
> Ordinary. She stands apart, is left alone.
> A widow (why no child?) and now a traitor's daughter.
> She knows what it means for her.
> This is a small town.
>
> ('Criseyde')

One wishes for more of this authority over existing sources. Both classical and medieval tragedy are especially self-aware, and the commentary on form, action and consequences within the poem (not just the introduction) is where Greenlaw's book succeeds – her story is a walled story within many walled stories, one that is (I would argue) less about love than about the pragmatic choices women make when rendered powerless by the male ego and their resulting demonisation. Troy itself is here a female metaphor. We even encounter Criseyde, in her circle of women, reading a "well-known tragedy" – the Theban cycle or some permutation. Fallen houses and fallen lovers *are*, as Greenlaw suggests, familiar stories into which we cannot but rewrite ourselves. But does the chronological re-plotting and summary re-reading of Chaucer and Boccaccio yield a new enough retelling in the twenty-first century? 'The art of poetry', a commentary on rhetoric, poetry and courtship, could serve both as the poet's own treatise on language and as a warning to would-be rewriters of myth:

> Use fine words but don't reiterate.
> Neither too neat nor too ornate.
> Don't spin arguments or put on airs.
> Use the right terms. This is love not war.
> Let an inkblot fall – like a tear.

Greenlaw's retelling attempts to remake without committing to either the past or present. But the story's several shared textual sources, its supposed love story, the iterative elements of tragedy therein and, ultimately, the lives of women (Cassandra appears in Chaucer's original and Helen is referenced elsewhere, as is Polyxena) ultimately deserve a bolder, more innovative approach.

Sandeep Parmar's debut collection, The Marble Orchard, *appeared from Shearsman in 2012.*

FURROWED AND STATELY

Rowan Williams, The Poems of Rowan Williams, *Carcanet*, £9.95
ISBN 9781847774521

reviewed by Patrick Mackie

. . .

Reviewing a book of reasonably good poems by someone that you passionately admire presents some nice conundrums. It is hard to get the angle of appraisal just right. Maybe some fusion of expectation and desire has made high demands of the poems, or maybe preference has crept in instead, and stopped them from being seen coldly or evenly. The poems are not the vast statements that the scale of the man might make us unjustly feel justified in seeking. But neither are they of anything like the slightness or mediocrity that would allow us merely to make allowances for a fine man's hobbies, while secretly wishing that he had spent the time on the main tasks for which we value and require him. Rowan Williams's poems live in exactly that twilight of quality where reviewing does not get to simplify itself into tones of either exultation or dismissal, and where substance emerges without really fleshing itself out into the fullest achievement. But the point is also that the poems do indeed live in that place, are alive in it and to it, and so vivify us through their awareness of their own rich conundrums.

One reason why it is possible to read these poems without constantly remembering their author has been Archbishop of Canterbury is he wore that role with the sort of distinction that does not insist on itself. Carcanet's book is in fact a reissue of a volume first published by Perpetua Press in the very year when he took on that vast and slippery job. The poems do not in any case directly record, or frontally assault, the issues of a career that was reaching towards such a public climax. But part of what makes the book so refreshing is Williams clearly never considered his poetry to be a separate enterprise from the grander or more grinding concerns of his life as a clergyman, a theologian and a bishop. 'Drystone', one of the book's first poems, comprises a lovely and tough little meditation on the drystone walls that criss-cross rural Britain, and is never less than rigorously focused. At the same time this rigour helps to make the poem into a little allegory, too, of what the book wants poetry to be, of the life of flexibly contoured immersion in a complex and sometimes blasted world that it wants its poetry to share with these "rough, bumpy" constructs.

So these are poems that want to track experience and the earth in all their swerves and abrasions. Lyric is here neither a refuge nor a source of merely high illuminations; it is more like a vantage point from which to survey experience or a resource within the tasks of sorting through it. An aptly rugged disposition for its craft is one marker of Williams's willingness to let poetry draw him further down and out into the world, rather than up and away from it. He is not exactly a virtuoso of verse forms, but then he is not interested in versifying as a vehicle for autonomous artistry or scintillating display. The capacious stanzas and the big, clumpy rhymes of 'Great Sabbath', for example, are touching because of the almost gawky fulsomeness with which they seek to match up to their subject matter. One stanza rhymes "dreams" with "screams", "earth" with "birth", and indeed "death" with "breath", and somehow, as the insistent and expansive monosyllables whack into one another, the effect is to convince us further of the poet's urgent interest in what he is saying. Williams has a feel for language that is sometimes tensely stringy and sometimes lapidary to the point of clunkiness. His voice is strenuous and often gaunt. If it is sometimes not entirely stringent, it also avoids the astringency that has come too easily to so many other high-minded poets in the crashing aftermath of Eliot and Pound. He wears his heart on a sleeve that he also rolls up.

Williams writes effectively about landscape because he has a humane grasp of its otherness as well as of its involvement with human stories. Any poem about Jerusalem has set itself a fierce and fraught subject, all the more so if its author is following a career like his. But Williams's treatment has freshness and density because it finds in its central image of limestone a different sort of topographical figure by which to broach the city's layers, so that its "powdered... chalky... dusty" world reinstates itself with vigour. His poems about paintings are rather less successful. Perhaps this only goes to prove he really is a poet, since poets tend to think they will write well about paintings, and they very seldom do. Williams's range of intellectual interests and competences is public knowledge by now, but it is still thrilling to see such seriousness of mind threading itself so unfussily and responsively through his poems. Few readers will be unaware how many fascinating and scholarly things Williams could find to say about Nietzsche if the fancy took him, so his treatment of the philosopher's years of mental debility gains poignancy and penumbra from its withholding of grand thoughts, its insistence on following its subject into the contracted concreteness of his decline.

In the end, the strength of these poems is in their sense of having patiently dwelled on and worried away at the large concerns of a lifetime, and at their best they have a music that is accordingly both exalted and grounded: "Passion will scorch deep in these sharp canals", so goes a line from a brief and lovely poem here about Bach's cello music, but the description fits Williams's style, too. His writing prods away at subjects with a meticulousness that is both furrowed and stately, and the feeling of slow release at its heart makes it hard to give a good sense of it in excerpts. But he is capable of such lines – or the one quoted below – that manage to clarify this patience within momentary but sturdy displays of iambic panache. 'Deathship', a longingly modest elegy for R.S. Thomas, closes with a small black boat putting out to sea, but Williams does not spell out its relationship to the dead man entirely, and the last line uses its pentametric throb, and the memories it evokes from within the poetic art itself, to instil a simple image with a rush of depth:

the boat flares in a blaze of crying birds.

British culture nearly gave itself a nasty shock when it put someone as gifted and demanding as Rowan Williams in such a central and resonant position. Of course, it managed to recover by more or less ignoring or misunderstanding what he tried to do with the job, and the Anglican communion did its bit, too, with its entangling controversies. It is good that this book has been reissued, and the publisher has pulled off a nice feat in making neither too much nor too little of the author's other vocation. A further volume of more recent material has been announced, so it may become possible sooner rather than later to begin to get a clearer sense of how independent of his larger life his achievements as a poet will seem in the end. The heartening thing about reading these poems now though, before their separate status can be steadily construed, is that they show what rich and wide nutrition a large and important public life can take from staying unseparate from poetry. Perhaps all the aspirants who throng our creative writing classes should be set the assignment of writing a poem from the point of view of an archbishop who is capable of forgetting that that is what he is.

Patrick Mackie's collection Excerpts from the Memoirs of a Fool *is published by Carcanet.*

COOL OIL AND SPEEDY TRAJECTORIES

Emile Verhaeren, Poems, *selected and translated by Will Stone*
Arc, £10.99, ISBN 9781904614692
Valérie Rouzeau, Talking Vrouz, *translated by Susan Wicks*
Arc, £9.99, ISBN 9781908376169

reviewed by Sophie Collins

. . .

There's an eagerness in Patrick McGuinness's preface to Emile Verhaeren's *Poems* to claim the Belgian symbolist as an optimist by nature. Initially, this is pretty difficult to go along with. After being led in fairly gently with the poem 'Baking Bread' – a gothic portrait of serving maids making the Sunday bread, their "sweat running into the mixture" – we're soon surrounded by "beads of blood and imprints of fury", literal baptisms of fire, hungry worms and rotting corpses, all fleshed out in unyielding blocks of text; tombstones on which are etched Verhaeren's visions and lamentations of a "dead Christian world". However, once adjusted to the sudden dark of the poems, their particular brand of "tender violence" – McGuinness's phrase – becomes somewhat more perceptible. Even in his most morbid moments, Verhaeren avoids any lapse into didacticism, and hope comes through in golden bursts, often in the form of the collection's most surprising and original images, as when industrialisation lights up "the tentacle town" like "an impassioned octopus".

Verhaeren's, then, is a deep optimism emerging from the honesty of his anti-idealist sensibilities, an awareness of the social realities of his time, of his own cultural duality and "the rich impurity of his language" as a Flemish writer, placing him "a world and a culture away from the transparent classical rationality of French". And this is what makes the poems so thoroughly readable: at his time of writing in the late nineteenth century, Verhaeren's work, with its propensity for free verse and spontaneity of expression, acted "like cool oil on the overtaxed alexandrines of French poetry". Today, in the context of contemporary British poetry, the lucidity of the translated poems has a similar effect, cutting through the horizon of familiar tropes with a hard intensity.

Will Stone doesn't go into his translation process. His introduction is an interesting but pretty staunch recount of Verhaeren's biography. But the book's blurb describes a "sympathetic modern translation", and certain things are obvious – the formal capitalisation of the beginning of the lines has been dropped, which superficially seems like a fairly minor innovation, but means that the enjambed lines that are there in the original are even more fluid in translation. Rhymes have been echoed where possible, but not in any systematic way, and so the translations avoid the pitfalls of this kind of dogged replication. There are a few particularly smart turns, as in the final line of 'The Crown', when "*Et sacre-moi ton roi souffrant et ridicule*" is translated as "and crown me your farcical long-suffering king", maintaining the presence of the hyphenation. Other great lines like "my science of boredom" come directly from Verhaeren.

A few decades before Verhaeren's time of writing, Baudelaire produced the first French translations of Edgar Allan Poe, and their influence on French symbolism is both deeply felt in Verhaeren's poems and neatly inscribed into Stone's translations. In 'Madman's Song' the cemetery rats "devour the worm that eats all / and their hunger lasts for evermore" – a broken echo of the raven's infamous refrain. This sense of perverse monotony is present throughout the collection, and continues even into the book's denouement, where it feels as though the more resolutely affirmative poems have been carefully aligned. However, in a collection whose aim is to allow the English-speaking world to return to the work of an important European poet, whose material has clearly been cherry-picked from a prodigious body of work and translated with heightened consideration for readers in the receiving culture, it was a bit of a thrill to encounter what is, for the most part, a bleak and uncompromisingly macabre gathering.

Susan Wicks's translation of Valérie Rouzeau is a completely different animal. The title *Talking Vrouz* reads and sounds like a mispronunciation of 'talking through', which makes me think of John Cage's conceptual 'writings through', and conflates also with "*vous*" (as in the French pronoun – 'you', singular or plural, but formal in the former) and 'vroom' (like a fast car). Collectively, these references would seem to form a gesture towards the outward-facing haphazardness of the collection, its whimsical but latently subversive tone and language games. Reading the translator's preface and notes, it emerges that we're not far off – '*vrouz*' is in fact a neologism attributed to the French actor Jacques Bonnaffé, describing the work in Rouzeau's *Quand Je Me Deux*, the earlier of the two collections that make up this book of translations. Rouzeau titled her next collection *Vrouz* to honour Bonnaffé's coinage, and it's these poems that occupy the second half.

The *Quand Je Me Deux* poems are the more familiar and the less interesting. 'Trr...' with its in-jokey dedication to the poet's immediate family puts me in mind of Muldoon's 'Quoof', and many of the poems in this first half are ruled by a similar nostalgia. For me, the real work begins in Part II with the *Vrouz* poems, in which Rouzeau seems to pose a challenge to the self-mythologising elements of the book's first half:

I'm good for this or nothing
Never learned to swim can't dance can't drive
A single car not even one that's small
Can't sew can't count can't fight can't fuck

These sonnet-length poems are described in Wicks's notes as "crazy self-portraits without self", and it's an interesting premise, to deal confession in terms of absence. The speaker is "nothing's rightful owner", "must lose fourteen pounds at least", and in dreams lies about her bra size. This deflection game is fun and often gendered in a very astute way. A real highlight of *Vrouz* is in some of the poems' truly brilliant final lines. Here are a few:

A big black empty vase of rainwater which hears.

Boom I've written signed my invoice note.

The big world without a feather daddy would go on.

While a sea-horse carries me away.

Dear Philip Larkin yes I'm also there.

The translations of *Talking Vrouz* are clearly devoted to their source texts. They do very well with the tone and rhythm of the poems, and also with the constant negotiations of Rouzeau's use of foreign phrases. However, the poems occasionally feel somewhat aged in translation, as when "*Je croise un beau garçon aux cheveaux blancs*" is made into "I cross paths with a dishy white-haired guy". The word "dishy" makes me recoil inwardly where something as simple as 'beautiful guy' would have worked well.

In her translator's preface, Wicks relates an all-too-familiar to-ing and fro-ing. A wish is expressed to preserve in some way Rouzeau's poems' "essence", located in this instance in the poet's "laconic tone", and her translator's approach is described as a slow arc from "necessary humility" to "daring" and "courage". Such an evaluation could in one way be said to reflect Rouzeau's poems' conscious distance from the hermeticism pertaining to much of French poetry, and in another come off as somewhat limited. If we take a view of translations as a way of reading the source text, it feels as though more attention could have been given to the receiving culture and these translations' position within it. I might compare *Talking Vrouz* to Jo Shapcott's *Of Mutability*, although really the newer pieces feel as though they belong to a subsequent generation, and it would have been interesting to see these converse with a range of upcoming American-influenced writers who share in much of Rouzeau's world, and her poems' knack for speedy, tingly trajectories.

Sophie Collins is writing a PhD on translation at Queen's University Belfast.

THE REPUBLIC OF DREAMS

John Ashbery, Collected French Translations: Poetry
Edited by Rosanne Wasserman and Eugene Richie
Carcanet, £19.95, ISBN 9781847772343
John Ashbery, Collected French Translations: Prose
Edited by Rosanne Wasserman and Eugene Richie
Carcanet, £19.95, ISBN 9781847772350

reviewed by David Wheatley

. . .

The small handicap of his writing in English notwithstanding, John Ashbery is one of the great French poets of our time. The heir of Lautréamont, Rimbaud and Mallarmé, he has reinvigorated that least English of forms, the prose poem; emulated Baudelaire and Reverdy's passion for poems about painting; been a New York School poet while living in Paris and a Parisian poet when back in the US; blithely bypassed the empirical worldview of the Anglosphere; staked his post-surrealist claim instead to what his mentor Raymond Roussel would call the Republic of Dreams; and generally lived by Rimbaud's injunction that *Il faut être absolument moderne.*

If, as Bunting said, assembling a *Collected Poems* is screwing together the boards of your coffin, what kind of realm have you entered when it's already a dozen years since you became the first living poet published by the Library of America? One of such sublime post-canonical ease that you can produce eight hundred pages of work you've done on the side, but that is still more impressive than most writers' *oeuvres* proper. Such are these two volumes of Ashbery's collected translations, in poetry and prose. Wallace Stevens thought that "French and English constitute a single language", but Ashbery, talking to Harry Mathews, expressed doubts about the two tongues' relationship. Stravinsky wrote his "sonata" for violin and piano, he declares, because he considered the two instruments incompatible and wanted to see if he could fix this problem; Ashbery feels the same thing when he brings English and French together.

"You take the form of a wave to make people think it's all the same to you", Ashbery's Jules Supervielle says in 'To Lautréamont'. Translation is not an overcoat a foreign text puts on against a change in the linguistic weather, but something altogether stranger and more fluid; compare Pound's distinction between "fluid" and "solid" form, and insistence that "some poems may have form as a tree has form, some as water poured into a vase". Like any free-flowing liquid, Ashbery's translations insinuate themselves into unexpected places. For some poets, dabbling in French translation means a lap of honour through the Panthéon, but Ashbery's subjects are much more unpredictable and in many cases as yet unheralded in English (Robert Ganzo, Armen Lubin, Maurice Blanchard, René Daumal and Marcelin Pleynet).

According to Walter Benjamin, the one category of text that cannot be translated is a translation. Ashbery adds a defiant twist to this in a series of versions of Mallarmé commentaries (*thèmes*) on English nursery rhymes, placing English and French text on a footing of equality – equally original or equally translated as the reader prefers, but not proceeding from any primary-secondary relationship. The results are sinuous little replicas of the author's prose poems, or rather both authors' prose poems, in a symbiotic pattern repeated in the selections that follow from Ashbery's 2011 version of Rimbaud's *Illuminations*. Of any other author, 'fluffy' could only be an insult, but where the French Ashbery is concerned the term acquires a joco-serious edge: the set of prose poems that follow, from Max Jacob's *Le Cornet à Dés/The Dice-Cup*, are steel candyfloss, twisting their conceits into place like tiny wire sculptures. Paul Valéry said he couldn't read novels because they all began with *"La marquise sortit à cinq heures"* (The marquise went out at five o'clock) or words to that effect, but if more novels began "On the Quay of Flames, the limping man drew my attention to the counterdeed, written in Chinese and in tiny letters", he might have rallied unexpected reserves of attention.

All writing aspires to the condition of translation. When George Moore suggested to the Gaelic League at the turn of the twentieth century that it publish a work of modern fiction in Irish translation, he wrote the stories of *The Untilled Field*, they were translated and then – the plan was – his originals would be destroyed. This last stage didn't happen, though the stories were re-translated into English from the Irish, prompting Moore to describe the results as "much improved after their bath". The discovery that not just the translated text but the original, too, exists in a state of self-estrangement is pure Ashbery, the "tapestry done in the form of a Möbius strip" that Helen Vendler has found in his work. A similar example occurs in Pierre Martory's 'Blues', whose French text is already a transposition of American speech patterns, but whose translation Ashbery does not garnish with imported American references, letting it come to rest instead on its adoptive terrain. In further elegant testimony to his rejection of myths of origin, there is even a section here of translations whose originals have been lost, including Pascalle Monnier's 'Luck is now sent to you...', which ends:

> kiss the one you love
> send 20 copies
> please
> see what happens
> don't keep this letter
> it must leave your hands

Dissemination is all. The second, prose panel of this two-volume diptych returns to some of Ashbery's touchstone authors (Roussel, Reverdy), turning up its share of curios such as Giorgio de Chirico's *Hebdomeros* and Artaud's agonised correspondence with the Jacques Rivière of the *Nouvelle Revue Française* (how many people write to *The Poetry Review*, I wonder, with news of the "cosmic breath of a soul shaken to its foundation"), and taking sideways looks at other art-forms in pieces by Henri Michaux and Iannis Xenakis. The Roussel section contains a letter quoting a couplet by Charles Cros that seems to have fuelled Roussel's extraordinary system of homonymic puns: "*Dans ces meubles laqués, rideaux et dais moroses / Danse, aime, bleu laquais, rit [recte ris] d'oser des mots roses*". This is translated as "Amid this lacquered furniture, these gloomy curtains and canopies, / Dance, make love, blue lackey, laugh to venture blushing words": a truly phonetic translation in the style of Zukofsky's Catullus eluding Ashbery's ingenuity, for once.

The first book Roussel published was a long poem, *La doublure*, meaning 'the lining' and, like Roussel, Ashbery is preternaturally sensitive to the secret alterities lurking within words. I've already used an aqueous metaphor for the act of translation, and the first poem in *Collected French Translations*, from Jean-Baptiste Chassignet, also begins with a meditation on water. Despite Heraclitus's warning, many poets feel able to step not twice but endlessly into his maxim on the unrepeatability of rivers. Seated "on the edge of a wavy river", our sonneteer warns, "you'll see nothing of the first wave". Ashbery's translations do not trade on nostalgic returns to the source; rather, they open a poetic channel in which first and more recent waves mingle as one. In any case, no nostalgia is required to experience the effect of these translations as peerlessly restorative and re-energising. In the words once more of Ashbery's Supervielle: "Around me I can plainly see the present year / And yet it seems to be the first day of the world."

David Wheatley's Mocker *and* A Nest on the Waves *are published by Gallery Press.*

Report

THE GLITTERING PRIZES

Joey Connolly investigates the culture of prizegiving

If the poetry world generated enough revenue to afford water-coolers and the grey-dappled institutional carpets for a space to gather, then the major poetry prizes would provide a perhaps discomfortingly large proportion of the chatter that surrounded them. One bubble in the easy flow of that conversation this year, though, would have concerned Fiona Moore's blog-post on the share of places on the shortlists for the Eliot and Forward prizes for best collection that are taken by poets from the 'Big Five': Faber, Carcanet, Bloodaxe, Cape and Picador. If we add the largest Welsh and Irish presses, Gallery and Seren, as well as subsidiaries of huge publishers, such as Chatto & Windus, then the figures are striking: ninety-three per cent of the Eliot shortlist and eighty-four per cent of Forward shortlist are made up of poets from these 'major' publishers. Given that these isles contain upwards of eighty poetry presses, need we be alarmed by such statistics undermining the genuineness of the claim of our prizegiving establishment to recognise the year's '*best* collection'?

Answering that question, we are faced with several possible responses. The first is to assent that this is a fair reflection of our publishing culture – the Eliot prize is right to conclude that in *every year* after its first, the best book of poetry in English has been published by one of five publishers. This is a difficult conclusion to come to for anyone wishing to attest to the vitality and variety of poetry in the UK and Ireland at the moment.

The second, voiced often and loudly, is that these prizes represent a closed system, with judges drawn from the lists of big publishers, and selecting in turn the work of their friends and colleagues; poetry being such a small world, it's easy to imagine that those very involved in it would be more familiar with the poems of those they know and work alongside (and familiarity can go a long way in the appreciation of poetry: if you understand the rules of a game, it's easier to know when someone's scored). Can we realistically expect those working in poetry – and possessing the profession's curious blend of insularity and empathy – to pass over books by those they know well? We needn't make any claim of corruption; aside from the familiarity and empathy for books by associates, judges are neither expected nor remunerated sufficiently to read every book of poetry published in a year. There's also the possibility that such ostensibly compromising links between judges and winners could well be often reflective of, rather than causal to, an admiration of a writer's work; people are friends (or colleagues, or supporters, or lovers) partly *because* they like the poetry of the other.

Despite these arguments, though, reading *Private Eye*'s 2002 dredging up of the sheer amount of links between judges and winners of the Forward Prize – the criticism at the time centred around a group of Picador poets, reviews in the *Sunday Times* and a shared agent, as well as social ties – is at the very least uncomfortable. There's an enormous amount of anecdotal evidence (unpublishably off-the-record, and quite often suspect) which won't suffice for making a case in accusations of cronyism, but which does nonetheless reflect a less-than-complete confidence in the impartiality of our judging processes. This concern is widespread: a survey of the editors of twenty-five of the country's independent poetry presses gave an average score of four out of ten in rating the success of the Eliot and the Forward prizes in recognising the 'best' poetry collections.

But a third possibility was put forward several times by those surveyed: that the poetry prizes aren't *seriously* intended to reflect the 'best' poetry being published. Rather, they're the one chance the poetry world has of attracting the notice of the mainstream media; an opportunity to bang the drum for contemporary verse, and to win new readers into the fold. It would seem that, as a corollary of this, the prizes become unable to honour strange or unusual work: genuinely original art cannot, by definition, be fully appreciated by the prevailing taste of the culture from which it emerges as original. Additionally, both the Forward and Eliot prizes employ a system in which the judges must agree on the winner, so that – unanimity being a decidedly scarce resource in the evaluation of poetry – a collection which is nobody's favourite gets chosen. It's easy to see how the safe option, to which there is no overly vociferous objection, all-too-often receives the prize.

There would seem to be, though, a certain pyrrhicism in the victory of winning readers to poetry if the work they discover upon their arrival is competent but unambitious verse lauded as the best our art-form has to offer. Indeed, it's the very competence of this kind of work which is its most dangerous feature; that is, being resolutely unobjectionable, claims of flawlessness can be levelled, and the valuable attributes of ambition, scope, originality and risk-taking become marginalised. Would readers newly initiated into such an art-form stick around? A counter-argument to all of this, of course, could be mounted by mutely pointing at recent winners: think of the fluid eco-phenomenology of Jorie Graham, or the endlessly surprising balance of delicacy and roughness by which Jen Hadfield confronts the natural world. Further, we might recall, and perhaps pay more attention to, the significant number of smaller prizes – often non-London based – which do tend to celebrate a much wider range of work.

The infuriating habit the world has of refusing a simple solution to such questions will suggest that the case is, as usual, a mixture of the proposed factors; the big publishers *do* publish many fine books, and poets tend to move across to those publishers as their work becomes more regarded (although this is by no means always the case). The poetry world *does* need its outside representation, and sometimes the friendly recognisable face of mainstream poetry might stand us in better stead with the as yet 'unpoetried' public. And, doubtless, as with the case *Private Eye* made disturbingly compelling in 2002, there are elements of (likely unintentional) favouritism and cronyism in the distribution of the prizes. It seems worth considering, further, that if we are to attempt to recognise something like the 'best' – that most poetry-retardant of terms – new work, then we have to accept that a certain set of criteria will be used in the ascertainment of such, and one enormous influence on such criteria will be the most visible and widely read books of the time. That is, the books published by the major publishers.

Even if we don't buy the 'closed-shop' argument, we nonetheless need to do what we can to defuse the criticism of our major prizes, and to ensure a credibility which can only reflect better on these prizes and their winners in the future. It seems natural at this point to steer the chatter around the water-coolers of the poetry world towards what might be done to disarm those who allege a bias in the prizegiving culture, and to heal what is undeniably a divide in the art-form's practitioners. More transparency would be a start – research of the kind this article required involved hours trawling archived internet pages, time that should for most be spent more happily reading poems.

Perhaps more transparency would lead to a widening of the pool from which judges are drawn. It is undeniable that the shortlisted poets and those of the judges that are publishing poets are drawn from the same circle, defined by the range of poetry presses around which they congregate. Going back ten years, of the Forward Prize judges currently publishing poetry, eighty-three per cent are published by major publishers – eerily close to the figure of the eighty-six per cent of shortlisted books originating with those presses. A case in point might be found in John Burnside, published by Cape (and previous winner of the Eliot, the Forward and the Costa, with several other shortlistings), who stepped down as a selector for the PBS just in time to be selected as its Spring 2014 Choice – meaning a place on the shortlist of next year's Eliot prize – and who has now stepped up to the plate as a selector of the next three seasons' Choices. Only one of the forty PBS Choices in the last ten years has come from a non-major publisher.

Even once this pool has been widened – the puddle at the foot of a water-cooler swelled to a mere with its shores far beyond the major publishing houses of London – the prizes could evidently do a great deal for their credibility by devising and implementing a code of practice for their judges. Why not require declarations of interest, both of the judges involved in the shortlisting process, and of those selecting the panels of judges? Why not lay bare the process by which these judges are chosen, and the shortlists assembled? Whether or not we agree that there are political and social undercurrents in the allocation of the Eliot and the Forward, it's clear that a little restoration work is needed on the faith the poetic community has in its major prizes.

Diary

EASTER IN BELFAST

Sam Riviere

Passover

I am writing to a German author I admire, or rather I am thinking of writing to him. I first heard his voice reciting a short story two years ago on an obscure American podcast. Since then his hesitant intonation and soft, precise lisp has installed itself in my mind's ear. Imagine these sentences spoken in an understated, reasoning German accent! So far this is all I have: "Dear Marcus, I've heard it said that the editing process is the only thing that separates the author from the work. All the behind-the-scenes rigging, the nights of toil and dark coffee, trimming and cropping, until it falls onto the page, complete, that smooth tonal effect, like a discarded skin, so easy to get into. I write to you from another rainy, walled city, wishing to make my voice as fully disclosed and undisguised as possible – a performance, of course, but one whose intentions have at least been transparently acknowledged. (While writing this the hiss of rain starts up at my window again, the wind scares itself sarcastically.) But let me get to the point. I would very much like for you to speak these fledgling attempts of mine, these days cast off, aloud, into a microphone (which if you'll allow me I'll provide) – Marcus, you may find my request too forward, but I'm given to believing in the Germanic approval of directness. Quite often now, I hear your voice in other novels. How to explain the attraction? Perhaps I feel my words would seem more authentically present in an accent that's a stranger to the language? If you agree, this would be the first piece you'd record."

Wednesday
Returning to the draft I'm preparing for Marcus, in a state of sort of hyperactive indecision, I feel paralysed by the sheer abundance of choices available to me. Under a spell of enthusiasm, I add copious, insignificant details about my situation, only to open the document again minutes later, press ←, and watch the cursor eat up line after line of my life. I'm stalled even over the question of whether to inform him of the country and city I'm writing from. Such are my impediments. Even some passing familiarity with my whereabouts could expose me as a falsifier.

Thursday
Someone (not me) seems to have stolen (Philip) Larkin's blue plaque.

Good Friday
Am I wired to see the object where there's only its suggestion? Are things really so pitiful? Any collection of shapes at the roadside can assemble the hitchhiker we desire. A girl in tiny denim shorts carries a mattress into a house. Chances pass on bicycles, plinthed high on bicycle seats. Who was it that said, *I want to heat the art.* The future's dark hair plumes, a mute, celestial face scanning rush-hour traffic for an entrance. She was all wrapped up like a Christmas present, but I hadn't the strength to unhitch the ribbon. A Spanish fantasy cruises past the clock tower. I've had eight already and I'm not full up... How do you handle it, Marcus, stick to the photographs? My eyes give me twenty lashes, each after-image collapsing like a dropped towel. The object was segued from this junk: a cack-handed composition of tinfoil, e-bay mirrors, monotony and Russian pop. It challenges you with a flick of its bangs, not mattering, total ghost burger, all of it.

Easter Saturday
The air is warm and full, hazy with droning bugs. The city reverts to a collection of barns... you can almost see the fields around it. The first day of spring, we took a political history tour in a black taxi. The driver's mic was turned right up, so we were able to hear sounds from outside at a strangely amplified volume. On a sunless estate a man pointed a stick at

a treeful of crows; their caws arrived loudly over the crackling system. Below the mural of Bobby Sands, back in the backseat, discussing the difference between the mural and film versions, the noises of an altercation reached us: our driver was in intense discussion with another driver, unseen from our position, whose vehicle had pulled up at a hasty angle. Words like "dispute" and "conviction" and "outcome" came over the speakers. There was a jostling sound, then our driver was climbing back in, adjusting his jacket, refixing his ID badge which had become dislodged in the struggle. As we inched along the curb, past murals depicting the conflicts of Israel and Palestine, the Basque separatists, Iraq and the USA, he explained the cab companies were riven by a long-running, internecine struggle, originating in the right of some companies to pick up passengers who hailed them, while others, arbitrarily it seemed, were forbidden from doing so. A committee had been set up to mediate the disagreement, though it wasn't long before it was discredited by the parties who perceived the injustice, and a second committee formed to monitor the first. Soon, the disagreements between the two committees became so turbulent, their views on each other's conduct so pronounced, that a third committee was required to mediate the first two; the third committee, though, quickly fell foul of the others, and in our driver's opinion was the first genuinely corrupt committee involved in the process. The third committee's well-known but publically refuted affiliation with the historically disadvantaged (or so they claimed) taxi operators inadvertently set back their own cause by four or five years, and relations between the first and third committees deteriorated to the extent that their respective members wouldn't sit down in the same room. The situation had now reached a point where a fourth committee was unfortunately necessary. The balancing of the fourth committee's representatives was clearly a task that demanded the most cautious handling imaginable. Our driver, at one of the regular meetings between recognised sympathisers of first and third committee members, who aimed towards a reconciliation of those now completely hostile entities, had voiced his disdain for the way the fourth committee was being assembled, a careless indiscretion for which he had just received chastisement.

Easter Sunday
Waking, I feel myself safely encased from the disturbed machinery in motion beyond my room. It takes a while to recognise the drums, like the

rhythmic sluicing of a giant washing machine on a high spin. From my pillow I can see part of a tree I don't know the name of, its twigs and leaflets frilling and jostling against whatever backdrop the sky provides – today a brisk, pale blue with gauzy strips of hardly-scrolling cloud. I lie in bed a while, rerunning what I can remember of my dreams, extracting a layer of translucent green film from each nostril; crisping quickly in the air, each holds the imprint of my fingertip. After a brief examination I flick the tiny, hardened shells to the floor and breathe in: I can smell cold air, carpets, something else calmly chemical. Perhaps my whole being is sealed by a similarly gelatinous membrane. If I could peel it away I'd be raw again, tender, touched by sunbeams, scoured by any slight breeze.

Easter Monday

Am I conditioned to perceive the threat where there's only its suggestion? Are things really so desperate? Any collection of shapes on the pavement can build the perpetrator I'm afraid of. Men lean on the bridge in threes. Who was it that said, *I want to meet the heart*. The future stood outside your house, a short figure in overcoat and gloves, and the whole ordeal unfolds again... The letters contained human hair and after a while I stopped opening them. A nightmare passed below your window, singing a wretched song. I found a pair of thick-rimmed glasses in the street, their lenses frosted white. A clear morning, nobody was up. The moon, reflected between chimney pots, stepped from window to window on the passenger side. A man waited in the shadow at a cash point. How do you deal with it, stick to the news reports? A car has been found. Constructed from debris, it is a cynical statement of counterfeit sentiment and demagoguery.

Earth Day

Still no reply from Marcus. I have moss on the mind.

Letter from Nicaragua

FESTIVAL DE GRANADA

Jane McKie and Jonathan Davidson

Jane McKie and Jonathan Davidson were invited as guest poets to one of the world's largest poetry festivals in Latin America's oldest colonial city

The tenth Festival Internacional de Poesía de Granada took place in the squares and outside the churches of Nicaragua's oldest city, from 16 to 22 February 2014 and was, this year, in honour of the Nicaraguan poet Rubén Darío (1867-1916), who is known as the "father of Spanish modernism". The lines from Darío chosen to adorn the 2014 programme are "Towers of God! Poets! Lightning rods of heaven...!", which perhaps goes some way towards introducing the flavour of the festival: declarative, flamboyant and passionately serious about writing. They might also strike one at first as absurdly inflated, pompous and certainly not of our time, but after a week's engagement with 141 poets from over seventy countries, the small, reluctant, emphatically British bit that loves to pooh-pooh grandiose statements started to crumble... *poetry is towering, is heavenly; we are becoming believers!*

The whole city was voluble. A small brass band had been set the task of providing a soundtrack for the festival and they popped up to serenade us poets wherever we went, and certainly contributed to our infection with the sheer joy of it and the concomitant laying aside of deeply ingrained cynicism. In fact, the chaotic mix of insistent Latin beats, heat, colonial architecture, nations, languages (although Spanish, rightly at this festival, reigned supreme), went a long way in a short time to unseat many prejudices. Chief among them was an Anglo-centric perspective on poetry, but perhaps more surprising was the melting of any resistance to idealistic statements about the power of literature to change individuals and society. We were, after all, in Nicaragua, where poets and writers play a central role in political life.

The previous year's festival had been in honour of Ernesto Cardenal, the Nicaraguan poet and priest who campaigned against the Somoza dictatorship and for "a revolution without vengeance", and who was Minister for Culture from 1979 to 1987 in the Sandinista-led government. At this year's festival he was again an honoured guest, at the age of eighty-nine cutting a distinguished figure and reminding us that he was a poet first and foremost. He was also proof, if it were needed, that in Latin America age and experience are still considered of value, especially amongst poets. While the young poets had a showcase reading in the festival and the daily 'open mic' was well used by those in their twenties and thirties, the deepest admiration was reserved for those in their sixties, seventies and older. Pedro Ávila of Puerto Rico, Jorge Arbeleche of Uruguay and the delightfully stern Harold Alvarardo Tenorio of Colombia were among the many older poets who brought the crowds to attentive silence during the evening readings.

Each year the festival adopts a different cause. This year it was dedicated to ending violence against women and girls, and the guests of honour included Pulitzer Prize-winner and former US Laureate Rita Dove, and Bianca Jagger, President of the Bianca Jagger Human Rights Foundation. Dove lent a regal presence to the proceedings, reading movingly and speaking eloquently about women's rights. Nicaraguan-born Jagger, too, was equally impressive on this subject. In addition to her foundation, she currently serves as a member of the Executive Director's Leadership Council of Amnesty International USA, a trustee of the Amazon Charitable Trust, and has vigorously campaigned on an extensive list of issues since the 1970s. The Nicaraguan novelist and poet – and another veteran of the Sandinista revolution – Gioconda Belli, was also a constant presence, as a member of the organising committee, as an important poet, and as a campaigner for freedom and equality.

Politics was most explicitly wedded to the festival in a midweek poetic carnival through the streets of Granada. It was a funeral procession for "male chauvinism and violence against women and girls", the idea of which languished in a flower-bedecked coffin inside an ornate glass-sided horse-drawn hearse followed by "parades of floats with all manifestations of Nicaraguan folklore". We walked from the atrium of La Merced Church, continuing along La Calzada, Granada's main street, to Lake Cocibolca where all the poets were led to a raised platform and honoured with crowns of paper flowers. Selected poets were given a chance to read at intervals along the route to crowds of people, including school children who – wonder of wonders! – earnestly asked anyone identifiable as a poet for their country, name and autograph. There was an ambiguity to our position: we were unknown and yet lauded just by virtue of sporting the poet's yellow wristband; it was perhaps a faint echo of what minor stardom might feel like, although we were very anonymous VIPs who could, for the most part, blend in and relax.

That outrageously colourful parade was an odd and humbling thing. When people asked to have photos taken with us, we couldn't help wondering about their histories, which might have involved real action as well as armchair activism. The folkloric costumes at the carnival ranged from dancers sporting the colours of tropical birds to twirling papier-mâché giants, and the humorous yet sobering witches and skeletons with pitchforks and scythes who ultimately bore chauvinism's coffin to the edge of the lake. It was a manifestation of the overturning of the everyday as well as a convivial public party. At its heart was the politically dissident mock burial as well as the crowning of fools, us poets who were kings and queens for the day, raised up on a podium and offered crowns, in a country where writers have little material status but are inextricably associated with political and cultural freedom.

So, alongside the jocularity – and the festival is jocular and inclusive – sits an avowed commitment to human rights. This was very much apparent at the dedicated evening of women's poetry, although, as Rita Dove observed, perhaps paradoxically, the event is as much about encouraging a culture in which differentiation along these lines is no longer necessary. Anat Zecharia from Israel read from her poem about the systematic abuse of a fourteen-year-old girl by thirty-five soldiers and several civilian employees at an airbase, called 'A Woman Of Valour' (translated by Lisa Katz): "A great love you think / a great love scorches me / and won't let up. / You raise and lower your arms / your body stretches to the edge of the sky / your hands cupped for the rain." Of course, not every poem was as explicitly political. But each was read as part of a common enterprise, a common striving towards the good.

The success of the festival owes an enormous amount to the enthusiasm of the poets involved. None of us received reading fees – although we were all exceptionally well looked after – and perhaps for this reason there was a sense of openness and equality. The Spanish-speaking poets in particular seemed confident in our collective status as 'poets of the world', helping even the most self-deprecating of English language poets feel that this art might be of some use and value. At the same time, we got the impression that Spanish language poets were not rushing to have their work translated into English, that their poetic centre of gravity was rightly hovering somewhere over the enormous reading and reciting landmass that is Latin America.

Our lasting impression is of the very natural relationship Nicaraguans have with poetry. The poet Francisco de Asís Fernández, President of the Festival, and Gloria Gabuardi and Fernando López, the Festival's Executive Organisers, represented this small country's selfless passion and this was matched by that of the audiences – often numbering over a thousand – who listened attentively each night. Although many in Nicaragua aspire to be poets, these were people of all classes and backgrounds who simply wanted to hear what the poets, above all others, had to say.

Thanks to Arts Council England, the British Council and Creative Scotland for supporting the authors' visit.

CONTRIBUTORS

Simon Armitage's *The Last Days of Troy*, a dramatisation of the Trojan War, is currently on stage at Shakespeare's Globe Theatre • **Edward Barker** was a prizewinner in the 2012 National Poetry Competition • **Mike Barlow** won the 2006 National Poetry Competition. His third collection is *Charmed Lives* (Smith/Doorstop, 2012) • **Colette Bryce**'s fourth collection, *The Whole & Rain-domed Universe*, will be published by Picador in September • **Harry Clifton**'s *The Holding Centre: Selected Poems 1974-2004* (Bloodaxe) is reviewed in this issue • **Joey Connolly** edits *Kaffeeklatsch* poetry journal. His poetry and criticism have appeared in *PN Review*, *The Rialto*, *Magma* and *Poetry Wales*. He received a Gregory Award in 2012 • **Jonathan Davidson** is a poet and radio playwright • **John F. Deane**'s *Snow Falling on Chestnut Hill: New & Selected Poems* was published by Carcanet in 2012 • **Carrie Etter**'s third collection, *Imagined Sons*, was published by Seren Books in March • **Alan Gillis**'s most recent collection is *Here Comes the Night* (Gallery, 2010). He teaches at the University of Edinburgh • **John Glenday**'s third collection, *Grain*, was published by Picador in 2009 • **Philip Gross**'s latest collection is *Later* (Bloodaxe, 2013). A new collection, *The Love Songs of Carbon*, is due next year. He received the T.S. Eliot Prize in 2009 • **Seán Hewitt** was born in 1990. He read English at Girton College, Cambridge, and is a postgraduate student at the Institute of Irish Studies, University of Liverpool • **Michael Hofmann**'s translations of Gottfried Benn, *Impromptus*, appeared from Faber earlier this year • **Jodie Hollander**'s pamphlet, *The Humane Society*, was published by tall-lighthouse in 2012. She lives in Washington, DC • **Sarah Howe**'s first collection is forthcoming from Chatto & Windus in 2015 • **Michael Laskey**'s fifth collection, *Weighing the Present*, will be published this autumn • **Gwyneth Lewis** writes in Welsh and English. *The Sparrow Tree* appeared from Bloodaxe in 2011 • **Kathryn Maris**'s second collection is *God Loves You* (Seren, 2013) • **Jane McKie** is the author of two collections of poetry and several pamphlets. She teaches at the University of Edinburgh • **Fiona Moore**'s pamphlet, *The Only Reason for Time*, was published by HappenStance in 2013. She blogs on poetry and poetics at displacement-poetry.blogspot.co.uk • **Conor O'Callaghan**'s most recent collection is *The Sun King* (Gallery, 2013). He teaches at Sheffield Hallam and at Lancaster universities • **Jacob Polley**'s third collection, *The Havocs*, was published by Picador in 2012 • **Sam Riviere** is the author of *81 Austerities* (Faber, 2012). His recent pamphlet, *Standard Twin Fantasy*, is available from Eggbox Publishing • **Susan Utting**'s latest collections from Two Rivers Press are *Houses Without Walls* (2006) and *Fair's Fair* (2012).

walk.
write.
pin

reveal

Poetry Pin is a geolocated digital repository for fresh and new site specific poetry, tethered to countryside west of the new nuclear build at Hinkley c in Somerset, UK.

come walk, come write, come read
open to all creatives

selected poems published
walks to inspire and meet other poets
2nd saturday of the month until march 2015

poetrypin.info

The Freud Museum and the Poetry Society present

MEMORY AND MEMORIALISATION
PSYCHOANALYTICAL POETRY FESTIVAL 2014
Saturday 27 September, 9am-5pm

Speakers and readers include
David Constantine, **Deryn Rees-Jones**,
Denise Riley and **Sam Willetts**.

There will also be a Festival reading at
the Freud Museum on the evening of
Friday 26 September.

The Anna Freud Centre, 12 Maresfield Gardens, London NW3 5SD
Tickets: £60 • £45 concessions • £40 Freud Museum/PS members

THE
POETRY
SOCIETY

Buy tickets at www.freud.org.uk

The Poetry Society at

POETRY INTERNATIONAL

Southbank Centre, London, 17-21 July 2014

Friday 18 July, 1pm, Clore Ballroom FREE
Poetry for secondary school pupils
Spoken-word artist **Joelle Taylor** introduces
an afternoon of young poetry collectives and
international poets for secondary school pupils.
Past winners of SLAMbassadors UK, the national
young people's spoken-word championship run
by the Poetry Society, take to the stage.

Saturday 19 July, 1.30pm
Clore Ballroom FREE
Creativity and Climate Change
World Premiere of the SWITCH Poetry Scores
Cape Farewell's poet-in-residence, **Sabrina Mahfouz**,
will introduce this world premiere of four unique
poetry soundscapes – an exciting collaboration
between four Young Poets Network poets and the
Hollywood composer **David Julyan**.

Sunday 20 July, 2pm
Level 5 Function Room, £8
National Poetry Competition Reading
Winners of the National Poetry Competition
including **Linda France** and **Tom Warner** will
give a celebratory reading. The poets will also
present a short discussion about poetry
competitions, and what makes a winning poem.

Book at www.southbankcentre.co.uk
or tel 0844 875 0073

THE
POETRY
SOCIETY *www.poetrysociety.org.uk*

ARTS COUNCIL
ENGLAND
Supported using public funding by
ARTS COUNCIL
ENGLAND

THE POETRY SOCIETY **ANNUAL LECTURE**

Carolyn Forché
The Poet as Witness

Photo: Don J Usner

AT POETRY INTERNATIONAL, LONDON

Sunday 20 July, 5:15pm
Purcell Room, Southbank Centre

Carolyn Forché presents the Poetry Society Annual Lecture at Poetry International, Southbank Centre, London, 17-21 July, exploring how poets have been shaped by extreme events.

From William Blake, caught up in the Gordon Riots, to Emily Dickinson living through the American Civil War, or Thom Gunn watching his friends die of AIDS, what has been the impact of being an eye-witness to suffering? Using the work of poets who fought on WWI battlefields, to dissidents who lived with surveillance, internment and exile, American poet Carolyn Forché examines poems composed at the limits of human endurance.

Carolyn Forché is Professor of English at Georgetown University, Washington DC, co-editor of the anthologies Against Forgetting *and* Poetry of Witness. *Her collections include* Blue Hour *and* The Angel of History.

Tickets: £10. Book at www.southbankcentre.co.uk or tel 0844 875 0073

AT FESTIVAL OF IDEAS, UNIVERSITY OF LIVERPOOL

Poetry & War: Carolyn Forché, Ilya Kaminsky & Brian Turner

Friday 25 July, 5pm-6.30pm
Abercromby Square
University of Liverpool

Carolyn Forché joins Brian Turner and Ilya Kaminsky at the University of Liverpool's Festival of Ideas commemoration of WWI. Supported by the Poetry Society, the event brings together three American poets in a rare UK reading, followed by a Q&A discussion exploring modern warfare, poetry and witness.

RSVP: http://poetryandwar.eventbrite.co.uk

 THE POETRY SOCIETY

 UNIVERSITY OF LIVERPOOL

 Supported using public funding by **ARTS COUNCIL ENGLAND**

The Poetry Society at
LEDBURY POETRY FESTIVAL
4-13 July 2014

Foyle Young Poets Award: Five Years of Winners
Sunday 6 July, 12pm, Baptist Church Hall
Event is free but must be booked in advance

The Foyle Young Poets of the Year Award is the key award for young poets aged 11-17 with over 7,000 poets submitting to the 2013 competition from all over the globe. This reading brings together winners from the last five years – **Philip Coales**, **Phoebe Power**, **Hattie Grunewald**, **Phoebe Walker** and Ledbury's own Young Poet in Residence, **Dom Hale** – to perform their latest work.

National Poetry Competition Winners
Friday 11 July, 12:45pm, Burgage Hall
Event is free but must be booked in advance

The National is the UK's biggest open poetry competition. Join three of this year's top winners: **Elaine Gaston**, **Josephine Abbott** and first prize winner, **Linda France** as they read their award-winning poems chosen from over 12,000 anonymous entries from 77 countries around the world.

Vew the Ledbury Poetry Festival programme at www.poetry-festival.co.uk

THE POETRY SOCIETY *www.poetrysociety.org.uk*

LEDBURY POETRY FESTIVAL 4-13 July 2014

THE LONDON LIBRARY

A rare haven for writers, poets and readers of all kinds.

The London Library in the heart of London's Piccadilly has been at the heart of the British literary landscape for over 170 years. Today it houses a unique collection of one million books, periodicals and reference material dating from the 16th century to the present day. It has long been a source of inspiration to generations of writers, poets and great minds alike. Prominent past members include Tennyson, George Eliot, Bram Stoker, John Masefield, Kipling, TS Eliot, Siegfried Sassoon and John Betjeman.

MEMBERSHIP BENEFITS

- 15 miles of books on open shelves to freely browse & borrow
- Wi-Fi equipped reading rooms & numerous quiet study areas
- Generous loan periods and no fines
- 2000 arts & humanities subjects in 50 languages
- Notable collections in Literature and Fiction with a substantial range of novels, poetry, plays, essays and literary criticism
- 750 magazine & periodical subscriptions
- Extensive electronic resources, including JSTOR
- Reference enquiries and research assistance
- Member offers & discounts at a range of organisations
- A postal loans service to anywhere in the UK and Europe

Annual & Gift membership is open to all for £39 a month (concessions available)

www.londonlibrary.co.uk

English Association Conference 2014

British Poetry of the First World War

An international centenary conference at Wadham College, Oxford

To book and see the full programme visit:
http://englishassociation.ac.uk/conference

🐦 @EnglishAssoc

Friday 5 - Sunday 7 September 2014 / Wadham College, Oxford

The English Association
www.le.ac.uk/engassoc

The English Association
University of Leicester
Leicester LE17RH
United Kingdom

📞 +44 (0)116 229 7622
✉ engassoc@le.ac.uk
🐦 @englishassoc
f The English Association

Visit our website:
www.le.ac.uk/engassoc

The Conference

An international conference to give all those with an academic or non-specialist interest in war poetry the chance to come together at the start of the Great War Centenary to listen to leading speakers and to exchange views about this body of literature.

Programme

The programme includes chaired discussions, 19 panel sessions and over 60 speakers, with keynotes from Edna Longley and Jay Winter. Jon Stallworthy, the conference patron, is guest of honour at the conference dinner on 6 September.

Day ticket prices start at £105.00 and the full Conference is charged at £325. To book and see the full programme visit http:// englishassociation.ac.uk/conference

ONLY YOU KNOW WHAT HAPPENS NEXT.

MA Creative Writing – Poetry

Our emphasis is the cutting edge of contemporary poetry. We combine dynamic, up-to-the-minute teaching with an open culture of learning.

Poets who have graduated from this course have published in high profile journals, won Eric Gregory Awards, won major competitions, been shortlisted, produced their own collections and gone on to develop growing reputations.

Study with award-winning poets Tim Liardet, Carrie Etter, Neil Rollinson and Gerard Woodward

How far can you go?
visit bathspa.ac.uk/pgwriting
or email t.liardet@bathspa.ac.uk

DIFFERENT THINKING